Dalit Paradigm

Dalit Paradigm

Concept and Theory Building

PRITI NATH SAXENA

RAWAT PUBLICATIONS
Jaipur • New Delhi • Bangalore • Guwahati • Kolkata

ISBN 978-81-316-0847-0

Published by
Prem Rawat for **Rawat Publications**
Satyam Apts, Sector 3, Jawahar Nagar, Jaipur 302 004 (India)
Phone: 0141 265 1748 / 7006 Fax: 0141 265 1748
E-mail: info@rawatbooks.com
Website: www.rawatbooks.com

New Delhi Office
4858/24, Ansari Road, Daryaganj, New Delhi 110 002
Phone: 011 2326 3290

Also at *Bangalore, Guwahati* and *Kolkata*

Typeset by Rawat Computers, Jaipur
Printed at Chaman Enterprises, New Delhi

Dedicated to

या देवी सर्वभूतेषु बुद्धिरूपेण संस्थिता।
नमस्तस्यै ॥20॥ नमस्तस्यै ॥21॥ नमस्तस्यै नमो नमः ॥22॥

(जो देवी सब प्राणियों में बुद्धिरूप में स्थित हैं,
उनको नमस्कार, उनको नमस्कार, उनको बारंबार नमस्कार है) ॥20–22॥

दुर्गासप्तशती सचित्र, गीताप्रेस, गोरखपुर (पृष्ठ 112)

Ya devi sarvabhuteshu buddhirupen sansthita,
namastasyai//20//namastasyai//21//namastasyai namoh namah//22//

—Shri Durga Saptshati Sachitra (page 112)

(English translation of Sanskrit verse)
That Goddess who abides in all beings as intelligence:
Salutations to Her ... again and again

and
Ravi (my husband)

Contents

Foreword

The 'rise and fall of equality' sums up the evolution of inequality and injustice. As Rousseau would say, *the first man who plotted out a piece of land and declared it as his own was the founder of civil society.* Modernity's passage through innumerable layers of time and countless ideological quagmires obscures our understanding of hierarchies that nourished inequality as an innate aspect of social evolution. But this critically is a simplification of functionalism that legitimizes both inequality and injustice. Sociologists, both Indian and Western, by and large, have followed this intellectually flawed logic.

Caste and its manifested proxies – *untouchability, Varna, Karma,* and *Dharma* – embody an impregnable system of institutionalized inequality. The basic tenets of our Vedic culture forbid praxis of liberation for the *wretched ones* at the bottom of social hierarchy. In this perpetuity of privileges and endless exclusions, we find marginalized humanity pitilessly exploited and oppressed in the name of tradition, which does not allow any upward social mobility. This closed, inflexible and intolerant system is fraught with *casteism* and its consequential 'caste war'. *Caste* is an ancient *class* system, which runs against cosmopolitan modernity. The pervasive dominance of an archaic system in the 21st century is a contradiction of democracy. There is a plethora of books and conference proceedings on the subject.

Dr Priti Nath Saxena has produced a trans-caste theory unravelling the *Dalit Paradigm*. *Dalitization* is a formidable challenge to the Brahman-Kshatriya-Baniya orthodoxies. Dalitization deconstructs Indian *pedagogy of the oppressed*; it encompasses dehumanization that blights all disenfranchised people, regardless of caste and religion. India's aggressively enforced and ambitious affirmative action, empowered by adult franchise, has radically changed the politics of caste. At its best, one of India's recent Presidents has been a Dalit. At worse, dalitization has engineered a 'caste war', which, functionally, blights merit, authenticity and excellence. It's a veritable movement in self-empowerment. This orientation marks a paradigm shift in our socio-cultural context, which harbours the world's most oppressed people. Democracies ought to unify and uplift marginalized people rather than drift them apart. Indian caste politics, however, thrives on fragmentation, which, unabashedly indulges in a pernicious practice of 'caste-ing' elections. Its own protectors pervert civility.

Social praxiological, *Dalitization* would de-castize Hindu culture, aesthetically opposed to Srinivasan's *Sanskritization* as it seeks to universalize the logic of oppression. 'Paradigm shift' underscores this interpretation.

Dr Saxena holistically examines variegated Dalit issues. While the significance of the Dalit paradigm cannot be emphasized enough, its viability as a transformational vehicle to change India remains debatable. Priti analyses the main issues in four broad categories: political elevation, neo-caste realist theory, Dalit philosophy (a trans-caste concept), eclipse theory, and conclusions. These planks constitute five chapters, logically woven around specified subsections. The analyses are coherently represented by a number of tabular structures and diagrams. The index, glossary and bibliography, significantly, enhance the impact of this no-nonsense treatise.

Zeitgeist seems to go beyond the theology of *Dalan*; human liberation remains eclipsed under ideological flux. Should a trans-caste paradigm become a reality, a new consciousness will have to replace the traditional vocabularies of Dalit and *Dalan*. Is India ready to embrace this challenge? I seriously doubt it.

There will never be a perfect and last word on a subject that is fraught with competitive morality and politics in a transitional society. However, any book so arduously written and organized by an expertly motivated author marks a transformative landmark. Age-old nihilism practiced with unabashed mythological exclusions will not go away with mere judicial and parliamentarian interventions. Nefariousness of a 'deep' state with creeping caste and class conflicts call for revolutionary zeal and indelible will of the people who are committed to self-transformation. In this direction, Dr Saxena's book is a positive step.

Brij Mohan
Dean Emeritus, LSU School of Social Work, USA
Founding Editor-in-Chief, Environmental and Social Psychology (ww.whioce.com); *International Journal of Comparative Social Welfare* (T&F); Chief Editor, Scholar's Pub. (Toronto, Canada). www.brijmohan.org

Preface

At the very outset, it would be pertinent to vehemently affirm that we, in India, not for nothing, are considered to be the most racist people in the world. This, of course, is due to caste discrimination. To unravel the crux of this issue, I have laid out a brief genesis of the Dalit Movement (DM) and have attempted to analyse it as one of the New Social Movements (NSMs). The sole purpose is to establish a paradigm of the Dalit concepts, its approach and theory. The focus is on an analysis of the movement, its past and contemporary phase.

At first, we will examine how the term (Dalit) is understood and second, what does it, holistically imply. Thus, an attempt is made to present a neo-Dalit epistemology, based on the ethical-philosophy of language. The latter is analysed in every sense to determine where and how the word Dalit can be implied and, thus, conceptualized in a new manner. Leaving aside the formulation of the term, a new social theory is offered to broaden an otherwise particularistic notion. As will be shown, it partakes of a universal scope, inclusive of groups à la social, political, economic, cultural and religious; also, it broadly encompasses all national boundaries. The trans-caste concept, in this book, is universal in scope. This concept generates more meta-ethical questions that are discussed in various chapters. It depicts how a particular social issue assumes a ground-breaking concept, relative to its social normativity.

By taking up a new, oft-ignored central issue of Dalit (in a sense other than caste), this volume attempts to create a new paradigm of the same. It is likely to create a new ripple in the philosophy of social stratification. Basically, it is a way to rethink and reflect the heterogeneity of the word 'Dalit', as opposed to a mere homogenous application. A heterogeneous approach focuses on the multifarious ways on how the term Dalit can be understood. Heterogeneity also affirms that this neo-concept of Dalit is in contrast to the old, classical and popular meaning of the term that is confined in a water-tight compartment of caste only. This is mainly due to the mindset of Indians. Finally, this approach leads to diversification in the meaning of the term trickling down to an individual's heart, mind and soul, and includes class, gender, polity, modern slaves and nature (the environment surrounding us) as discussed in Chapter 3. It implies that up until now the general comprehension of the term Dalit has been limited to the lowest level of the caste hierarchy, which is considered the 'true' notion. This volume is an attempt to build a theory based on a wider or universal meaning of Dalit.

Our universal, empirical understanding of the concept and theory addresses the relevance of the subject on a trans-caste level. By doing so, the focus is a less particularistic to more generalistic view, that is, from understanding the politics of an individual's mind to a nation's mind.

It attempts not to a mere explanation of Dalit/*Dalan*/oppression, but to explain the interplay between domination and repression through various examples. The book not only analyses the domination of and by the powerful, but also focuses on the repression faced by the oppressed/Dalits. Hence, both micro and macro understanding of the concept are covered.

Through this paradigm of concept and the New Social Theory (NST) – derived thereafter (based on both hypothetical and empirical analyses) – my attempt is to make my viewpoint (on the term Dalit) be understood by my readers in a Platonian metaphor. It means Dalit or NST of the Dalit based on capital 'D' – 'Dalit' and not 'dalit', as such.

I hope this book – with an inter-disciplinary touch – will not only benefit academicians, research scholars, writers, analysts and students – interested in the area of polity, society, philosophy, linguistics, history (and its aligned disciplines à la social-philosophy, political-philosophy, political-sociology, political-history) but also political leaders and party workers. The NST explains the practice and exercise of dominance and extreme suppression by trans-caste means in various ways. It also explains how and to what extent those adversely affected feel the pulse of oppression. It is through this prism of NST that an attempt has been made to build a new Dalit epistemology as opposed to the classical one (based only on caste). This indicates that both *Dalan* and Dalit is a universal phenomenon prevalent among all human beings in the world. The direct corollary of this would be how can we change the knowledge system of a given set of people. This refers to the meaning of Dalit as understood by upper-caste peoples in India.

The domination versus oppression praxis, based on the trans-caste philosophy, can lead to a new model of the latter (discussed in Chapter 3), which is likely to attract attention of both Indian and foreign scholars. This is because as discussed in Chapter 3, the universalization of the concept of Dalit and *Dalan* and the new paradigm built thereafter, one can find innumerable examples of Dalits in the world today. It is in this sense that the neo-broader concept of Dalit holds importance specially in the sense other than caste.

Priti Nath Saxena
(pritinath493@gmail.com)

Acknowledgements

I cannot but express my heartfelt gratitude to my father, late Tribhubhan Nath, a veteran Chandigarh-based journalist who had walked the corridors of the University of Allahabad, for his unqualified support throughout my life. My mother, late Sarla Nath, a Delhi University meritholder and lecturer, had worked cheek by jowl with my father in sowing the seeds of literacy in me. Under their unflappable wings, I could safely tread the academic path to excellence.

I couldn't have been luckier to get in touch with Prof. Brij Mohan, Dean Emeritus, School of Social Work, Louisiana State University, United States, who spared some invaluable time to write the foreword of this book. Thanks to Usha Shrivastava from the Social Work Department of Lucknow University for her unstinted support. I am extremely grateful to Prof. Mark Lindley, a well-known international scholar from the United States who needs no formal introduction – for his valuable academic inputs which were of great help in improving the script. I am highly indebted to him for introducing the theme of my book to readers.

My special thanks to the special man in my life, Mr. Ravi Saxena (Senior Corporate Executive), my husband, for his unbridled support and cooperation in completing this book. My sister, Tripti Nath, a senior Delhi-based journalist, unwaveringly supplied me with the related material vide e-mail with regularity for which I am grateful to her.

My heartfelt thanks to Shri Radhey Shyam Sharma, ex-editor, *Dainik Tribune*, Chandigarh, Meena (a banker at Wells Fargo, United States) and Kanta Singhania (Chandigarh-based academician) for their moral support.

I would also like to thank Prof. Sudhir Sharma, Professor of English, lyricist, script writer and composer from Bollywood, for smoothening the rough edges in the language, if any, and to Mr. Sohan Lal Sharma for typing this manuscript very patiently. And of course this list of acknowledgement would be incomplete without naming Shri Pranit Rawat of Rawat Publications. His prompt replies and suggestions were a great help in publishing the script. I express my deep regards and thanks to him too.

Finally, I would like to submit that I have tried my best to eliminate errors and still is there is any error in the text then it is purely unintentional. I will be happy to accept it and hope that readers would excuse me for the same.

Priti Nath Saxena

List of Abbreviations

AAP	–	Aam Admi Party
AIDWA	–	All India Democratic Women's Association
AIPWA	–	All India Progressive Women's Association
AISCF	–	All India Scheduled Caste Federation
B	–	Brahman
BAMCEF	–	Backward and Minorities Community Employees Federation
BJP	–	Bharatiya Janata Party
BKD	–	Bharatiya Kisan Dal
BSP	–	Bahujan Samaj Party
CBI	–	Central Bureau of Investigation
CM	–	Chief Minister
DC	–	Dalit Consciousness
DIC	–	Dalit Intellectual Activity
DM	–	Dalit Movement
DM	–	District Magistrate
DP	–	Dalit Panthers
DS–4	–	Dalit Samaj Shoshit Sangharsh Samiti
EBCs	–	Extremely Backward Classes
IDSN	–	International Dalit Solidarity Network
ILO	–	International Labour Organization

ILP – Independent Labour Party
ISIS – Islamic State of Iraq and Syria
K – Kshatriya
MBCs – Most Backward Castes
MNCs – Multi-National Corporations
MP – Madhya Pradesh
n.d. – Non-dated
NFIW – National Federation of Indian Women
NGOs – Non Governmental Organization
NSMs – New Social Movements
NST – New Social Theory
OBCs – Other Backward Castes
PC – Post-Colonial
PD – Political Distance
PM – Prime Minister
PP – Political Parties
RPI – Republican Party of India
S – Shudra
SAD – Shiromani Akali Dal
SC – Scheduled Castes
SCF – Scheduled Caste Federation
SEP – *Stanford Encyclopedia of Philosophy*
SNDP – Sri Narayan Dharma Pripalana Yogum
SP – Samajwadi Party
SP – Superintendent of Police
STs – Scheduled Tribes
UCP – Upper-Caste Parties
UN – United Nations
UP – Uttar Pradesh
US – United States
V – Vaishya
VHP – Vishva Hindu Parishad

List of Hindi Words

Hindi word	English translation
Abhijan	Minority/elite
Abhiyan	Movement
Adidharmi	Religious minority
Andolan	Movement
Antim	End
Antyaja	Last in caste hierarchy
Asharam	Disciple-teacher residence
Asthirta	Unstable
Ati-shudra	Untouchable caste
Avarnas	Last in caste hierarchy
Bachao	Save
Bachpan	Childhood
Badla	Change
Bahishkrit	Denounce
Bahujan	Majority
Bhageedari	Participation
Bhakti	Devotion
Bhangi	Untouchable caste (Sweeper)

Bharat	India
Brahman	Upper most caste
Bundele	Name of community
Chakki	Grinding machine
Chashme hakikat	Real view point
Chaudhary	Indian surname
Chor	Thief
Chowk	Crossing point on four lanes
Daav	Strategy
Dalan	Oppression
Dalit	Lowest in caste strata
Dalitva	Twice born (upper caste)
Dekho	See
Dhoondo Mat	Don't find
Ek	One
Ghad De	Fabricated
Ghrana	Hatreke Drshti Se
Guru	Teacher
Gurukul	Old school system in India
Harbole ne	Everybodys' view
Hein	Is
Hindustan	India
Idhar	Here
Jalkari	Dalit woman soldier
Jati	Caste
Jhanda	Flag
Jhoothi	False
Jitni	As much
Kahani	Story
Khalasi	Name of a post
Ki	Addressed to his/her

Ko	Addressed to his/her
Kshatriya	Third in caste hierarchy
Laxmi Rani	Queen of Jhansi
Mahar	Untouchable caste
Majdoori	Lobour
Makaan Banata Hai	Builds a house
Mali	Gardener
Manuvadi	Followers of Brahmanical caste system
Mat	Vote
Na	No
Nahi	No
Nahin	No
Naye	New
Nirbhaya	Fearless (also name of the movement)
Nishan	Mark
Or	Towards
Pahchan	Identity
Pandits	Upper most caste
Panja	Hand
Panth	Religious system
Prakar	Type
Prarthna	Prayer
Ravidassia	Name of caste
Raj	Rule
Rajneik	Political
Ran	War
Rigveda	First of four old Hindu religious scriptures
Sab	All
Sahitya	Literature
Samaj	Society

Samiti	Committee
Sankhya	Number
Sarv	All
Sarvjan	Everybody
Satyagraha	Movement for truth
Satyashodhak	Purification of truth
Shiksha	Education
Shasan	Administration
Swarna Jatiyan	Upper Caste
Swatchata	Cleanliness
Tantrik	Exorcist/one who indulges in black magic
Tasveer	Picture
Udhar	There
Utni	As much
Vaishya	Third in caste hierarchy
Varna	Caste
Verrane Mei	In deserted area
Vikas	Development
Yaron	Friends
Yojna	Planning
Yug	Era

1

Political Elevation of Dalits

Mohi tohi, tohi mohi antar kaisa

—Ravidas

(between thou and me, me and thou
how can there be a difference)

Some of the best indications of the internal world of 'untouchables' in India emerge from the literature of *bhakti*,[1] a so-called 'devotional' movement. This movement for banishing the deprivation of Dalits and discrimination against them had its beginning in the 19th century. Much has already been written on how it spilled over, gradually, in different forms into various regions, until it created a national-level awareness among the lower castes in the 20th century.[2] Among its few well-demarcated castes, the top three – Brahman, Kshatriya and Vaishya – respectively attend to society's spiritual, defence and trade needs, leaving the menial jobs to the Shudras – the fourth category called untouchables. They cremate the dead, collect nightsoil and the like to subserve the top three categories. As the society's underdogs, they have been given different names in different periods in various parts of India. Their identity at the lowest rung of social hierarchy has had a religious and historical sanction. They had to undergo a punishment for no fault other than their birth in the lowest strata. They have themselves been accepting their low-grade caste status. However, this position was not acceptable to free India, at least on paper if not in actuality. Independent India's Constituent Assembly called a halt to this unjust social discrimination by promulgating a constitution recognising by legal force the principle of equality – social, political and economic – to all its citizens, regardless of caste and religion. In effect, it abolished all kinds of discrimination overnight (as it came into force on 26 January 1950), associated with the notorious untouchability prejudices. It is true that the Scheduled Castes' protest against social oppression took a new turn as India's Republican constitution drafted by Dr Bhimrao Ramji Ambedkar became operative on 26 January 1950. Yet, untouchability is still alive and kicking, albeit in a subtle form.[3] This social bias is far from being uprooted as evident from recurring incidents of violence against the Dalit caste people – the weakest section of society. While suffering insults, humiliation, oppression and discrimination, the untouchables have had to content themselves with accepting their servile position. They had no all-India organisation to agitate their cause.

The core issue is what is the root cause of discrimination[4] as experienced by Dalits vis-à-vis its sociological set up?[5] One cannot ignore the fact that the origin of the caste system is centuries old, and its laws are very strict. The laws are so strict that the social system became entrenched in our nation's minds through generations.[6] Sometimes, it assumed the ugly form of atrocities against the downtrodden people. The Constitution's protective provisions remained only on paper, a token of good intents. It failed to produce a dramatic, let aside produce a revolutionary change in the overall conditions of the Dalits. It was high time now for the Dalits themselves to raise their banner of revolt. This, however, remained a scattered effort, as distinct from an organised, all-India movement. Beginning in the southern and western India, it gradually spread, considerably later, to northern states – Punjab, UP and Bihar when it had already challenged the authority of higher castes (Savarnas or Brahman ruling class) in south and west.By recounting the historical background of Dalit Movement (DM), this book hopes to make a major contribution to frame a New Social Theory (NST) based on intertextuality. Although caste identity is the basis on which this study has been developed,this has been made only in a peripheral manner, treating it as a socio-cultural heritage. The main thrust of this study is to build a trans-caste concept and theory. In order to understand this in a holistic way, political elevation of Dalits in India has to be analysed through review of relevant literature. Caste has, by and large, become a mindset of Indians. Progressive legislation and constitutional safeguards have done little to rid the social order of the widespread evil of caste discrimination.[7] Both Edmund Burke and Kumud Pawde's quotations support this view. The hierarchical structure of the Indian society described by Edmund Burke is as follows:[8]

> In that country the laws of the rule, the laws of the land, and the laws of honour, are all united and consolidated in one, and bind a man eternally to the rules of what is called caste.

Stating the fact that caste has become a mindset of Indians, Kumud Pawde feels: '... although I try to forget my caste, it is impossible to forget'.[9]

What are the problems that the issue of caste has created in our society? What kind of discriminations have the Dalits faced in the past and what are their present problems? What is new about the political representation in North India over the past two decades vis-à-vis problems of Dalits? What have Dalits gained from the electoral process in India? What have they contributed?[10] These questions assume significance since there is now a clear evidence that Dalits vote numerically more than and more differently from other sections.[11]

Will the Dalits always have to remain content with the demand for such job reservations, 'which effectively means that they be employed as proletarians in the enterprises owned by others – in primarily upper caste concerns or those owned by the state but nevertheless, controlled by the upper castes? Should they not also have their own bourgeoisie? Their own millionaires and billionaires?'[12]

Does the Hindu traditional social order, in its classical form, come in direct conflict with the universal human rights framework and how the continuation of the practice of caste system and untouchability in modified forms lead to the ubiquitous violation of human rights, particularly the Dalits?[13] Do cultural, social, religious and economic notions make the enforcement and practice of human rights difficult?[14] When Dalits, backward classes and most backward classes taken together constitute a majority of India's total population, what would be their impact on its (India's) future and vice versa?[15] What can be the impact of globalisation on socio-economic relationships? Can globalisation open the door of opportunity for Dalits?[16] How can Dalits get guaranteed participation?[17] These are some basic questions that constantly raise our curiosity. The core issue is what is the root cause of problems the Indian society and politics faces vis-à-vis the traditional idiom of caste today?

In the opinion of Ramashray Roy:

> Most of the people belonging to Scheduled Castes, caught as they are between obtrusive past and elusive present ..., caught in this vicious circle, they suffer from an acute feeling of frustration and alienation.[18]

Untouchability is the most extreme mode of punishment to the downtrodden for no fault other than their birth among the lowest strata of society. They were deprived from birth from social and economic resources let aside power and/or privileges.[19] What did they inherit? Other than poverty, misery disease, unemployment and hunger.[20]

Devabrata Bose's study depicts and condemns the menial and degrading occupations.[21] From the pariah, an untouchable's shadow was considered polluting by orthodox caste – Hindus. Till present day, the journey of lower caste has been troubled, contradictory and painful.[22] A few studies have brought out significantly the root cause of discrimination as experienced by Dalits? What problems has the Indian society and politics faced vis-à-vis its sociological set up in the past and what are its present problems? Undoubtedly, untouchability of the lowest strata of society all over the country during the colonial era was the most challenging problem causing fragmentation of the nation.[23] It was considered totally incurable.[24]

In fact the social, economic and political status of a shudra in the pre-colonial and colonial era was based largely on upper castes' faith in Manusmriti.[25] The following quotes prove the point:

> Nothing at all belongs to a shudra at his own. He is one whose property may be taken by his master.[26]

> And one may not teach him (shudra) the law or enjoin upon him religious observances ...[27]

> A shudra is like a burial ground ... therefore, Veda be never recited in his presence ....[28]

Interestingly, there is a remarkable universality about this problem the world over.[29] For instance, the American white masters did exactly the same as our Brahman masters did to their 'labour pool'. In the New World (USA), they made biblical knowledge a taboo and learning a crime for them.[30] Indeed, Munshi Premchand's 'Sadagati' of the pre-independence days, in which a Dalit dies of thirst, hunger and slave-labour, continues to be enacted in our moral hinterland like a haunting tragedy.[31] Taboos imposed by the tradition and misbelief still exercise their stranglehold over Indian society. The Dalit community is forced to accept social obligation and economic deprivation, as borne out by surveys conducted across four Indian states.[32] As Simon Charsley and G.K. Karnath observe: 'Untouchability, is legally forbidden yet it is alive, though perhaps not kicking'.[33] Even today, in many villages they are denied access to drinking water available only in public wells. They continue to be treated as bonded labours.[34]

A national English daily *The Hindu* carried prominently a report from Mehboob Nagar district of Andhra Pradesh, describing a dispute on drinking water or tea from the same glasses as used by upper castes in tea shops.[35] Even now in some areas of Andhra, U.P., Bihar and Madhya Pradesh, the people from Scheduled Castes cannot ride their bicycles across an upper caste villages.[36] This was because their shadow is still considered polluting for the upper caste people. Another glaring example and caste discrimination can be gauged from the well-known columnist, Sainath's article:

> Welcome, to the 'two-glass' system close to half-a-century after the abolition of untouchability, serving 'polluted' people in separate vessels is a common and widespread practice. In Kanmanur, says Elappa, a Dalit resident of the village, 'every tea shop has a two-glass system. No only that, the barbers here also refuse to trim our hair. And, the Harijans cannot enter temples even today ...[37]

This kind of discrimination on caste lines was also found after their death. As Sadanand A. Shetty observes –

> ... According to a press report (*The Hindustan Times*) in Ukinath, bodies of 32 villagers belonging to Scheduled Castes, continued to rot for more than a week since the rescue workers, majority of whom were from the upper castes refused to touch them ...'[38] It may also be noted that in some areas Dalits still cannot enter temples of upper castes. Reports say that in Nathdwara in Rajasthan, there is this unwritten law that no Dalit can enter upper caste temples.[39] In Orissa ... in most temples, the gates are still shut for 'pariahs'.[40]

In feudal Andhra, Dalits cannot draw water from the same well or bathe in the same ghat with the upper castes.[41]

Besides, casteist violence in UP does not spare even children.[42] It was also reported that 'two Dalit families of Uttar Pradesh pay the price in blood for defying their upper caste neighbours, and the state government apparently ignores the incident'.[43]

Moreover, in the state where a Conference (Madhya Pradesh) was held for the economic upliftment of Dalits, Scheduled Tribes were attacked in forest areas.[44]

According to an inquiry report on Kambalapalli carnage (*The Hindu*), the state was noticed colluding with the dominant castes in several areas in all the states and it fails to implement all the laws for the protection of Dalits.[45]

A noted scholar on Dalit problems observes: 'The condition of Dalits at the village continues to be vulnerable under decentralisation of power. Elected representatives from the Dalit community, more often than not, do not have any say in village affairs'.[46]

In addition to the problems of untouchability, violence and discrimination briefly touched above, it would be relevant to take note here of other problems (during the pre-colonial and post-colonial) that led to the emergence of Dalit issues. The problem of political deprivation is discussed in the following paragraphs.

Caste system has served as the backbone of Hindu social structure for a long time. Indian history reveals how various communities were separated into endogamous groups, that is, jatis (castes). The topmost in the caste ladder was the Brahamans (B), who were the priestly class and performed religious rites only. The second in the order was the Kshatriyas

(K), who were the warriors and were supposed to protect people. Next to them was the Vaishyas (V), who were the merchants or the peasant classes and their work was confined to business or trade. The lowest in strata was the Shudras (S), who were assigned menial jobs and it was also their duty to serve the B, K and V. Thus, each caste had a traditional and hereditary occupation. It remains so even today as one can see that it is a part and parcel of the Hindu culture. The words caste and varna[47] were, many a time, used as synonyms. Though varna means colour, the underlying connotation was so strong that classes came to be regularly described as varnas, or four different colours were supposed to be the distinguishers between them.[48] Technically, it meant nothing, but it helped in befooling people into their old system. Moreover, many restrictions were imposed upon the Shudras.[49] The ill effects of a hierarchical caste system have prevented the fruits of development from reaching the large majority of Dalits. This largely explains the conditions of poverty, exploitation and deprivation experienced by Dalits.[50]

In order to understand the history of caste, it is also important to understand what roles the shudras were assigned by the original law givers: Panini and Manu, during the Rig Veda period. Despite the contrast of their views, that is, the former's assertion that castes were the offspring of Vaishya-Kshatriya and Vaishya-Brahman marriages, respectively, and the latter declaring that they were residents of Magadha and Videha. The important point is, how did the people who had no stigma attached at the time of Panini became so stained in the hands of Manu?[51] A study by Nandu Ram states that Ambedkar believed that Manu could not be regarded as the originator of the castes nor could he have been given the law to it because 'castes existed long before Manu'.[52] Instead, Manu upheld and philosophized about it. Rigveda also mentions the shudra only once and that too at the last stage of the hymns.[53]

It is this stigma of untouchablity that Dalit faced that led to an evolution of various anti-caste movements in different phases of history. Most supporters of these movements, whether in pre-colonial, colonial or post-colonial period, tried to answer the question of origin and problems of untouchability. In this context, for instance, the modern Dalit-Bahujan movements, while building up an anti-caste ideology, drew upon the dialectical materialism discourses that started in a proto-materialist form from the Indus based Lokayatas or charvakas who continued to operate all through history. Lokayatas were the earliest Dalit-Bahujans who fought against the Aryan invaders. They gradually established the Brahmanical socio-political and economic system in India.[54] This was followed by the opposition that came from the Jain and the Buddhist schools. Whereas the former preached total non-violence against the violent, the latter emphasized the Lokayata view.[55] During this period the major point of debate, revolved around the questions as to who were the shudras, what was their origin.

Various studies prove that in many parts of India shudras had been rulers and slave-owners. The 'Buddhist literature speaks of Shudra kings ....'[56] As regard the question whether the vedic varnas constitute a class or caste, studies reveal that the vedic varnas constitute a class system, not a caste system. Central Hindu values expressed in the Rig-Veda could do without the Jati system. Among 'these values there is first of all Rta, the world order.'[57] Akin to 'Rta', there is Satya, truthfulness.[58] In the Bhagwad Gita, the link between truthfulness and vocation or worldly function is explicitly made in the notion of Swadharma.[59] While not describing a casteless society, the Mahabharat is not objecting to it either.[60]

About the origin of untouchables, one theory is that the untouchables were originally 'Broken Men', people who had been isolated from the community, through expulsion from or other ways.[61]

The details of the origin of the untouchability and the racial ethnic composition of the scheduled caste population are shrouded in mystery. '... we trace its origin from the vedic period, i.e. coming of Aryans in India during 2500 B.C. to 2000 B.C. and from the writing of Rigveda ...'.[62]

The Adi-Hindu movement propounded the theory prevalent at that time among depressed classes in certain parts of the country that the 'achhuts' or untouchables were the original inhabitants of India and in the pre-Aryan era had possessed large kingdoms, cities, forts and a thriving civilization.[63] 'The Aryans came from outside or invaded India ... the dwijas among them were whites; the Shudras the original inhabitants of India were dark.'[64]

On the other hand, it is opined that the origin of four 'varnas' is grounded in myth that is, different 'varnas' owe their origin to different parts of Brahma, creator in Hindu concept.[65] It is generally argued that the caste system came into existence 4000 – 4500 years back.[66] The widely popular theory traces it to the Aryan invasion of this country.[67] While this is the most accepted view, it is also pertinent to note here Purnendu S. Kavoori's opinion:

> The evolution of castes including the forming of 'varna' ideology was a historical consequence of economic system development. The emergence of untouchability is seen as an ecologically determined adaptation contributing to the fitness and survival of those regarded as untouchables.[68]

The medieval period, however, ushered in the Brahman control of society. It was in the discourses of Krishna that we find post-Bahujan resurgence. In the late medieval period, Islam provided relief to the Dalit-Bahujans as it believed in social equality.

Thus, during the 13th and 14th centuries, conversions to Islam,[69] Christianity and Buddhism brought about some kind of relief to the Dalits, but not in toto. One can trace chronologically that Ramanuja, Basava, Inaeswar, Chokhemela, Kabirdas, Eknath and Sri Narayan Guru were all an integral part of anti-Brahmanical movement in order to earn self-respect for the Dalits.[70] However their religious reforms could only marginally affect the age-old problem of untouchability.[71]

In a reference to the life of depressed class people, Oliver Mendelson observes:

> If literary evidence suggests that untouchability had entrenched itself by the second century of the present era, the details of the untouchables' lives are remarkably sketching until the modern speriod. But some of the best indications of the internal world of untouchables emerge from the literature of bhakti, a so-called 'devotional' movement sometimes dated as far back as the seventh century but whose main influence has exerted for some 500 years from the eleventh century.[72]

For some scholars, the voice of Dalit Liberation had its genesis in the *Bhakti* period, à la Kabir saying:

> Pandits sat and read the law
> Babbled of what they never saw.[73]

Sometimes more images were painted in words, and they were addressed directly to the upper castes *Jis Tan Lage Vahi Tan Jane Duja Kya Jane,*[74] which means only the sufferer can understand the pain of suffering well. This particular *doha* reflects an epistemological point which firmly legislates that 'the consciousness of suffering can occur only to those who actually suffer from victimhood', as observed by Gopal Guru.[75]

> Between thou and me, me and thou, how can there be a difference, said Ravidas, an eminent thinker and reformer.[76]

Ghanshyam Shah observes: 'Chokha Mela (14th century) a Dalit Bhakta from Maharashtra, had the agony of his oppressed position in society. He sometimes revolted against it and sometimes accepted his position as a reward of *karma*. He said–

> If you had to give me this birth,
> Why give me birth at all?[77]
>
> One of his 'abhanga' ends thus
> In the beginning
> At the end
> There is nothing but pollution
> No one knows anyone who is born pure
> Chokha says, in wonder,
> Who is pure?[78]

Chokhemela (14th century), a Dalit Bhakta from Mahrashtra, suffered the same agony. He, sometimes, accepted his position due to his belief in the Karma theory.

Although a follower of his illustrious father Chokha's son Karma Mela could be blunter and more bitter.

> You made us impure
> I don't know why Lord.[79]

The theological boldness spilled over into the society thinking of bhaktas like Kabir, but it is not possible to make out a strong case for their constituting a revolutionary movement.[80]

It was not only tameness of ideology that limited their impact rather *bhakti* was to a large extent appropriated and assimilated into orthodox Hinduism.[81]

According to Chandra Bhan Prasad and Sheoraj Singh Bechain:

> There is growing tendency amongst non-Dalit scholars to talk of Dalit rights rather passionately, but at the same time, debunk their movements and leadership. This has happened with the Nirgun Branch of the Bhakti movement and it was repeated during Ambedkar's movement. Once the movement fades and the leaders depart, the same movement is glorified and the leaders eulogised.'[82] The feeling that welled up in untouchable and low-caste communities during the most productive phase of bhakti can surely not have simply ceased to exist. But what we can say is that 'it was not until developments of the British period that a fresh ideological attack could be mounted against the principle sustaining untouchability. This new challenge enjoyed circumstances for more favourable than those of the bhakti poets.[83]

In the modern period, the liberation movement started following a Brahman sepoy's refusal to lend his *lota* to an untouchable *khalasi*. The sepoy had his objection to giving his *lota* to an untouchable.[84]

The feeling that welled up in the untouchable low-caste communities during the most productive phase of bhakti can surely not have simply ceased to exist. But what we can say is that it was not until the developments of the British period that a fresh ideological attack could be mounted against the principle sustaining untouchability.[85] This new challenge enjoyed far more favourable circumstances than those of the bhakti poets.[86]

In the subsequent decades of the 19th century,[87] this awareness of their being castaways led to organized efforts to gain self-respect. They were led mainly by Jyotiba Phule, Baba Saheb Ambedkar, P.V. Ramaswami 'Periyar' Narayan Swami Guru, Achutananda and Mangoo Ram.[88] In this context, B. Krishna Reddy observes:

> The conflict between Harijans and caste Hindus can be understood as follows: the state of the dalits is complex, as it is a product of socio-cultural, economic and political factors. If things have to change, an analysis of the way, social forces interact is to

> be launched – Harijans have felt the need to fight the atrocities launched – Harijans have felt the need to fight the atrocities perpetrated on them by the upper caste Hindus.[89]

The conflict between Harijans and caste Hindus can be interpreted in terms of W.G. Ogburn's concept of 'cultural lag' which explains that some aspect of culture (non-material aspects of culture) do not undergo change so fast as do other (material aspect of culture) and hence, there emerges a 'lag'.[90]

In the words of Ghanshyam Shah:

> Identity formation calls for sharing of a common culture, on the one hand, and harping on the separateness from others, on the other. Efforts were made by untouchable leaders early in the 20th century to carve out their distinct identity from caste Hindus. It was asserted that untouchables constituted a *quam*, that is, community like those of Muslim, Hindus and Sikhs, having their own religion and culture.[91]

It was Phule who first addressed the problem of untouchability and tried to organize the non-Brahman groups against the Brahman dominance. He was the founder of Satyashodhak Samaj and used the word 'Bahujan'[92] for the first time. He also used the words 'Shudra' and 'Ati-shudra'.[93] Later his efforts culminated in a movement of the Bahujan Samaj versus Shetji-Bhatjis[94] in Maharashtra. Phule advocated Bali Rajya as opposed to Ram Rajya,[95] as the former was a shudra ruler who did not allow caste distinction to affect job position. He felt that modern Brahman Rajya of the Congress, headed by Tilak, could never solve the problem of untouchability.[96] He believed there could be no integration in the nation as there was a lot of inter- and intra-caste distinctions, such as between Aryabhat Brahmans and Mahars[97] on the one hand and ignorant Shudras and the latter on the other hand. Phule also became the 'guru' for Dr Bhimrao Ramji Ambedkar (popularly known as Babasaheb Ambedkar). Ambedkar talked not only of untouchables' oppression but also of violence and exploitation that the peasants faced. Another pre-Ambedkar leader was Kisan Faguji Bansode, a Mahar journalist[98] of Nagpur who asked Aryans to stop the harassment of the oppressed people. But the movement by Dalit leaders remained confined only to the Maharashtra region. As Gail Omvedt observes:

> Phule also realised that an alternative Indian culture had to be created as a mass culture. Yet his voice remained a regional one, limited to Marathi, its influence hardly spreading behind Pune district in his own time, while the Indian National Congress of the Brahmanical elite established its organisation throughout India. Phule failed. The non-Brahman movement could not move beyond gaining a share of power for some of the non-Brahman elite ....'[99] Besides, it was mainly a movement for creating 'self-respect' for untouchables.[100]

In the words of C.P. Bhambhri:

> P.V. Ramaswamy Naicker launched a big renaissance movement against Brahmanical Hindu ritualised religion and achieved a lot of success in liberating the oppressed castes in Tamil Nadu from the ideological control of Hindu religion.[101]

In Tamil Nadu, P.V. Ramaswamy Naicker[102] launched a movement for the oppressed, which he termed a 'self-respect movement'. They tried to build pressure on the government to bring about social egalitarianism, what has been termed as 'Dravadian' identity. In the end, reservation was not simply granted reluctantly but granted in a way that seemed almost designed to sabotage its purpose.[103] 'Scheduled Castes' and 'Scheduled Tribes' were to be let in, but there was an effort to ignore as far as possible the claim of the 'other socially and educationally backward classes'.[104]

Gail Omvedt observes: 'Periyar brilliantly made 'self-respect' a mass movement, building up a peaceful force involving activists drawn from all castes and from both men and women. And, in projecting a 'Dravidian' identity and rooting it in what was perceived of as the culture of the Tamil people, he succeeded in giving a powerful thrust to the mass-based social alternative'.[105]

In this context V. Krishna Ananth observes: 'Periyar treated social reforms and political mobilisation as two separate aspects. Such an approach was, one can say with the benefit of hindsight inherently flawed. Periyar may have had his compulsions at the stage'.[106] The story of how the nationalism of E.V. Ramaswamy and Ambedkar are suspect even today.[107]

In Gail Omvedt's words: 'Yet the Dravidian movement also failed in establishing itself as an alternative to the 'Vedic Aryan

Brahmanic' force it despised. Not only did it lose its radical social thrust, which would have included the liberation of women and full human rights to the Dalits, it remained confined to Tamil Nadu. In focusing on Tamil national identity, the concept of 'Dravidian' civilizational identity was lost. By falling victim to racist/chauvinist attitudes towards 'north Indian' as a group and 'Brahmans' as a whole, the Dravidian movement in Tamil Nadu condemned itself to remaining a sectoral force, powerful in its homeland but harped even there and severely handicapped in contributing to an all-India liberatory movement'.[108]

At the time when Phule was propounding his radical attack on caste in Maharashtra, Sri Narayan Guru (1857-1928) was developing a comparable but simultaneously religious critique that was widely accepted even beyond his own Ezhava community, in Travancore.[109] By 1891 there were already some 25,000 educated Ezhavas in Travancore, and 13,176 of them signed a petition in 1896 to the Maharajah asking that government schools and the civil service be opened up to them.[110] This movement also remained confined to Tamil Nadu and was powerful only in its homeland. In the later 19th century, Narayana Guru[111] made efforts to ask for admission of Ezhavas into government schools and to get an opening in the civil services. Sri Narayan Dharma Paripalana Yogum (SNDP) was formed for the amelioration of Ezhawas. Narayana Guru (who was also known as Sree Narayana Guru and an Indian social reformer) belonged to Ezhave family (Kerala), which was considered as an outcaste (avarnas in Hindi). He and his followers built temples which were open to the untouchables. His aim to build temples (in Kerala and Karnataka) was to get rid of caste superiority by upper castes (Savarnas) and to break the exclusive monopoly of Brahmans in the temples.

At that time, the only Mahar political organization in existence was V.G. Walangkar's 'Anarya Dosh Parihar Samaj' (Society for the Removal of the Stigma of Untouchability).[112] Vithal Ramji Shinde of Maharashtra argued for better representation of each caste in the legislature. The low caste leaders persisted with their efforts to find a solution to the problem of untouchability in their own ways.[113] On 11 November 1917 under the chairmanship of the late Sri Narayan Chandravarkar the depressed classes held a meeting and the chairman of this public meeting was authorized to request the Indian National Congress to press at its forthcoming session a distinct and independent resolution, declaring to the people of India at large the necessity, justice and righteousness of removing all the disabilities imposed by religion and custom on the depressed classes.[114]

The early Mahar movement, before 1920 is comparable in a number of respects with the single caste movements of the Ezhavas, the Nadars and Pulayas of South India, and also of other communities such as the Namsudras of Bengal.[115] This inclusive position was taken a step further in a movement throughout south India which sought to construct their identity by creating the untouchables as the original, pre-Aryan inhabitants of India.[116]

In this context, an analysis will be relevant, in short, of the efforts made by *dwija*-caste leaders. Thus, efforts were made by the oppressed caste leaders for the lower castes, but these remained sporadic and single caste movements.

Efforts were also made by *dwija* caste leaders. Raja Rammohan Roy endeavoured to remove the evil of casteism through *Atmiya Sabha* and later *Brahmo Samaj*. However, he had no clear-cut programme to accomplish his goal. B.G. Tilak addressed the first Depressed Classes Conference held in Bombay,[117] but ultimately, gave primacy to *Swaraj*, that is, political reform over social reform.

Both Raja Rammohan Roy's *Brahmo Samaj* and Justice Ranade's *Prarthna Samaj* could not jointly make a dent in the caste orthodoxy.[118] Both moderates as well as radicals did not want to overthrow the Hindu social system as such as is evident from the following statement. What they wanted was to 'lop off the diseased overgrowth and excrescences and ... restore vitality and energy to social organism'.[119] A host of other leaders behind the movement included Dwarka Nath Tagore, Devinder Nath Tagore, Keshav Chandra Sen, Ishwar Chandra Vidyasagar, Swami Dayanand, Swami Vivekanand and Shri Aurbindo. Unfortunately, their perception about the caste system is a view from a *dwij*-lens, that is a higher plane.[120] The Brahmans are called *dwij* because it is believed that they are twice-born people who enlighten the other three castes in the social ladder. Therefore, some critics believed that since the aforementioned names of leaders (who made some efforts to erase untouchability) were from the *dwij* caste they could never offer an unbiased viewpoint because they had never faced the problem of untouchability in their personal lives. Hence their viewpoint was from a higher plane.

Ambedkar and Gandhi espoused different positions on the issue of untouchability. While Gandhi maintained that caste had entered in the past without untouchability and the former could be purged from caste system without doing damage to the latter, Ambedkar considered the abolition of the caste system as indispensable, for he thought the outcastes would be outcastes as long as there were castes. He felt that untouchability was like a nausea of one group against another.[121] In his Marathi fortnightly, – the *Mooknayak,*[122] he addressed two issues. The first was untouchables' rights, and the second was how the latter could be achieved without obstructing national goals. His efforts[123] included the *Chavedar Satyagraha*, the formation of *Bahishkrit Hitkarini Sabha*, the public burning of Manusmriti, and active participation in Round Table Conferences.[124]

To Gandhi, Harijan was a better term than Antyaja. In the Sanskrit language, Antyaja means 'one who is last-born'. On the other hand, Harijan means 'men/children of God'. Hari in Hindi means 'God-Vishnu' and Jan (again in Hindi) means 'people/children'. Gandhi felt that by calling Dalits Harijan ('a child of God.'), we could change the mindset of people and bring about equality in society. This is what he espoused in his weekly publications and through his non-profit organization, Harijan Sevak Sangh. Harijan Sevak Sangh is a Hindi word, and its English translation means 'organization for the service of untouchables' (Dalits). It was founded by Gandhi in 1932 to eradicate untouchability and to improve the quality of life for Dalits. Gandhi started a weekly journal in three languages on 11 February 1932. *Harijan*, was the name in English; *Harijan Bandu* in Gujarati and in Hindi. Initially, the organization was called the Anti-Untouchabiity League, which helped Dalits to access public places such as temples, schools and roads.

Gandhi believed, 'The touch-me-not-ism that disfigures the present day Hinduism is a morbid growth. It belongs to a woodenness of mind. ...'[125] Though Gandhi was against the practice of untouchability, one finds his firm belief in *varna* duties in one of his quotes: 'The Brahman's duty is to look after the sanitation of soul, the *bhangis* that of the body of society.

Apropos Gandhi's views on caste and intermarriage, Mark Lindley observes, 'Gandhi's views in regard to basic aspects of the caste system changed in the last years of his life'. In the 1920s he had held that every Hindu 'must follow the hereditary profession' and that 'prohibition of intermarriage' between people of different varnas was 'necessary for a rapid revolution of the soul'. Later he became 'a social revolutionist', advocating intermarriage between Brahmans and untouchables in order to dismantle the caste system 'root and branch' and acknowledged that 'When all become casteless, monopoly of occupations would go'. The changes were due in part to the influence of two opponents of the caste system whose integrity he held in high regard: Ambedkar and Gora.

Lindley further states: 'Historians know (and any sophisticated person would suppose) that Gandhi's status as a Mahatma – great soul did not prevent him from changing his mind about some things. Many people in India know, however vaguely, that for most of his life he did not campaign against the entire caste system but only against some aspects of it (and especially the doctrine and practice of untouchability)'. Politically sophisticated observers have occasionally remarked that his intellect was far more complex than his clothing.[126]

In fact, the historic Poona Pact[127] became a bone of contention between Ambedkar and Gandhi. It was due to the moral blackmail exerted by Gandhi's epic fasts that Ambedkar signed the Poona Pact in 1932. Despite this controversy between them, their roles were indubitably complimentary to each other. While Gandhi's special concern for untouchables manifested itself in seeking after improvement in their standard of living, Ambedkar's programmes were intended to integrate the untouchables into Indian society in modern and not traditional ways, and on as elevated a level as possible.[128]

As to the efforts to resolve the problem of untouchability, Ambedkar was dissatisfied with the British, the Congress and the intelligentsia's approach.[129] He felt the depressed classes have had no friends[130] and the government, all along, used them only as an excuse for prolonging its existence. It is important to mention here colonial sociology,[131] especially the status of untouchables. The problems of untouchables were not confined to them alone but, in a holistic sense, they weakened the nation.[132] This can be better understood in three ways. One, the British Government challenged the credentials of the Congress to represent the entire nation. Two, in the 1881 Census,[133] the British Census officers were focused on answering who happened to be a Hindu. The British Census officers wanted to know whether Dalits were Hindus or Hindus comprised only the three upper castes of social hierarchy. In this way, the British were only trying to take advantage of this caste division in society by imposing a question on Congress as to how it was representing the nation minus Dalits. Three, the colonial government stoically continued to rule India by taking cover in the argument that they could not afford to share or abdicate power when the social grounds for power sharing were shady.[134] Ambedkar had a strong opinion regarding Hindu social order, self-respect, Dalit Consciousness (DC) and conversion to Buddhism. In order to solve the problem of untouchability, Ambedkar said, 'Political power is the key to all social progress'.

Ambedkar's leadership against caste oppression led to his attempt to form the first political party for the lower castes in the 1930s. Independent Labour Party (ILP) was a worker and peasant party with a red flag and Dalit leadership. It participated in the provincial elections held in 1937 for the Bombay Presidency. While it won major successes (both electorally and in terms of leadership in mass movements) in the Marathi-speaking districts, it failed to make an impact at the all-India level. Ambedkar replaced it with a new party: All-India Scheduled Castes Federation (AISCF) in 1942. It focused on Dalit autonomy and made a poor show in the first general elections. Ambedkar, himself, was defeated by a Congress Harijan candidate. Ambedkar decided to wind up the

Scheduled Caste Federation (SCF) and reformed it into a broad-based party in 1956.

In between this period, India witnessed a Dalit movement in many states by various leaders,[135] such as in Bengal where Shivnath Shastry worked for the depressed classes mission and tried to educate them. Swami Vivekanand tried to awaken the ignorant masses through the Ramakrishna Mission, which was formed in 1896. Also Thakur Hari Chand started the Matua sect and was the pioneering leader of the untouchables. Other notable movements were in the former Central Province, which was a province of British India and covered parts of present day Madhya Pradesh, Chhattisgarh and Maharashtra states. Guru Ghai Das, Gangaramji Dhuldhoye, Shakarro Ramji Madji and R.L. Jangde were the leaders from Madhya Pradesh, who worked for the betterment of Dalits. In Kerala efforts for the same were made by Shri Narayan Guru, Changaram Kumarth Krishnan and Kalappan. Nirban Chandra Mukherji, Prakash Chandra Roy and M.S. Roy made pioneering efforts in Bihar. In Maharashtra, Bombay and Gujarat, Balshastri Jambhakar, Phule and Ambedkar made major contributions, while in Karnataka it was Jyothi Dass. In Punjab, it was mainly the efforts of members of Ahmadyia Sect: Arya Samaj and Radha Soami Satsang. In Uttar Pradesh, members of the Hindu Backward Classes League, Brahmo and Arya Samaj, Kabir and Ravidas Panths made every effort to put an end to untouchability. In Andhra Pradesh, the Dalit leaders were Kandukuri Veersalingam Pantulu and Bhagya Reddy Verma. In Orissa, Kanlur Charan Jena and Moan Nayak worked to improve the conditions of Dalits, and in Rajasthan it was Dayanand Saraswati who tried to change the mindset of upper castes vis-à-vis Dalits. In Tamil Nadu, members of the Self-Respect Movement, Justice Party, and Diwan Bahadur M.C. Rajah made efforts to improve the conditions of Dalits.

The aforementioned efforts to uplift the depressed classes remained more or less a social reform movement. What did Dalits gain out of this? Any political benefits? This is crucial to comprehend the post-colonial Dalit movement.

Initially, the political benefits were confined only to the efforts of Ambedkar who was included in the first cabinet of free

India as a Law Minister on 15 August 1947. Articles were framed dealing with untouchability and reservation and welfare of SCs, such as Articles 17, 330, 332, 338, 339 and 340.[136] It was through the efforts of Ambedkar that an exclusive party of the Dalits, the Republican Party of India (RPI)[137] was formed to fight for the equality of all Indian citizens by ensuring special consideration to the Dalits to build up a balanced society. However, in the 1960s, the RPI was divided into several factions and was unable to make much headway into politics as the party was too localized. Some of the members had also been co-opted into the ruling party at the state and central levels. Except for winning a few seats here and there, it was not able to make much headway in politics.[138]

Analysing the case study of Charmakars, B.V. Bhosale states: 'The RPI claims to be the care-taker of Dalit movement and Dalit politics but it has not given any representation to Charmakars in party cadres and elections. This party has remained exclusively of Neo-Buddhists or Jai-Bheem Walas. The RPI has failed to mobilise Charmakars'.[139]

In 1970 with formal split of the RPI, two factions emerged, one openly favouring the Congress policy and getting co-opted with it, while the other maintaining its distinct identity.[140] Through its persistent demand the RPI was successful in getting the government to pass the Protection of Civil Rights Act, 1976.[141]

The RPI failed to make an impact at the national level for four reasons:

> The party was 'too weak and localised (Maharashtra) and even in those pockets its ranks were not united, the party in power commanded the resources to extend patronage to the aspiring Dalit leadership through the policy of protective discrimination. These leaders emerged as serious challenge to the RPI leaders; the party did not have an ideology or an action programme radically different from that of the other parties that had begun espousing the Dalit cause; and the RPI leaders were often been co-opted into the ruling parties at the state and central levels, thereby eroding the potentiality of the party for any serious and sustained mobilisation of Dalits.[142] However, just before Ambedkar's death, he formed Samyukta Maharashtra Samiti,[143] which demanded the creation of a separate Marathi-speaking state in 1956 out of the

then bilingual state of Bombay. Meanwhile, similar alliances were formed in Tamil Nadu, Karnataka and Andhra Pradesh.

In the next phase of Dalit politics, the Backward Class (BC) movement was emerged, which focused on identifying the backward and 'more backward' communities and make recommendations for their advancement. Mandalism,[144] which had its progenitor in the Dravadian movement, also initiated special efforts for admissions in public educational institutions and reservation[145] of jobs for lower castes. 'Mandalism' loosely refers to the Mandal/Backward politics in India. The Mandal Commission was established in India in 1979 by the Janata Party under Prime Minister Morarji Desai to identify the socially or educationally backward people. It was headed by Indian Parliamentarian B.P. Mandal. Through this commission, the focus was to give exclusive access to members of lower castes: OBC (Other Backward Classes), SCs (Scheduled Castes) and STs (Scheduled Tribes)[146] to jobs and education. Policies were drafted and implemented to these ends in 1953, 1961, 1977 and 1990.

In a comment on the next phase of development in Dalit politics, T.V. Rajeshwar wrote:

> Mandalism had its prognitor in the Dravidian movement in the south which was basically against the domination of the Brahmans in all walks of life.[147] Before going further into the details of Mandalism, it would be pertinent to note a brief history of backward classes, its definition and what the free state of India proposed at the time of independence.

For Phule, Ambedkar, Periyar, Shahu Maharaj and others,

> reservation was not simply designed as a kind of helping hand for the oppressed but as a part of a broad and visionary attack on a system of exploitation. The first actual implementation of reservation system came in 1902 when the ruler of Kolhapur state and descendant of Shivaji and Shahu Chattrapati, issued a government order that from then posts in his administration should be filled with candidates from any communities except 'Brahmans, Passis, Shenavis'. This broad-scale reservation policy was aimed not simply at providing a form of social mobility for non-brahmans, it was designed as a blow at the concentration of administrative power in the hands of upper caste communities.[148]

However, the Indian Constitution or the Indian freedom struggle did not contest particular identities with universality – it promised universality despite the socio-economic particularities.[149] Reservations were aimed to help an individual transcend the disabilities imposed upon him by the social stratification of a traditional society.[150]

It would be pertinent here to understand the phrase 'socially and educationally backward classes'. Perhaps referring to the ex-Shudras as Scheduled Castes the new usage seemed to provide an opening – although throughout the British period, terms like 'Depressed Classes' and 'Backward Classes' had invariably been used to refer to 'jatis'.[151] The term 'reservation' serves several purposes – it allowed the elite to maintain the façade of a generous patron of Dalits and Adivasis which continuing to deprive them of mass-level education and access to resource.[152]

According to M.N. Srinivas 'The first such commission was appointed in 1953 with a respected Gandhian, Kaka Kalekar, as its Chairman, and it submitted its report in 1955. It listed 2,399 communities as 'backward' and with 837 of being classified as 'more backward'.[153]

In August 1961, the Government of India intimated the state government that while they had the discretion to apply their criteria to discretion to determine backwardness; it would be better to apply economic tests rather than go by caste. This position, however, went against the general trend of judicial interpretation of the constitutional provision regarding reservation for the 'socially and educationally backward classes'.[154]

In 1977, Morarji Desai appointed a Bihari leader, late B.P. Mandal, to head a Commission to identify BCs and make recommendations for their advancement. The report submitted by him in 1980 was neither implemented by Indira Gandhi nor Rajiv Gandhi.[155]

In August 1990, V.P. Singh pre-empted the OBC vote-bank by announcing the implementation of the Mandal Commission recommendations, reserving 27 per cent of jobs in the Central government for the BCs.[156] This caused a big stir in the Hindi heartland inciting many young men from the upper castes to commit suicide by setting themselves on fire.[157]

M.N. Srinivas quotes,

> Professor B. Sivaramayya, a legal scholar has carefully analysed the judgement in '*The Mandal Judgement: A Brief Description and Critique*'. The judgement declared that 27 per cent of jobs in the Central government and public sector undertakings be reserved for 'Other BCs', that the total quantum of reservation not exceed 50 per cent and finally that the 'creamy layer' in each backward caste be excluded from reservation.[158]

Referring to the politics of identification, Pradeep Kumar states:

> The politics of identification is an important aspect of Dalit politics. There are three principal reasons why this is so. Firstly, the benefits of reservations are inherited which means that once an individual got the benefit of reservation because he belongs to an identified caste, the benefit is likely to be continued ... secondly, the entire caste qualifies for the benefit ... thirdly, the backward communities are not homogeneous and they constantly fight with each other ... example Madigas and Malas.[159]

Thus, politics of identification is an important part of Dalit politics. The BC movement and Mandalism provided a stimulant to bring caste more to the forefront of the nation's consciousness.

Between 1972-1976 there were other movements that helped consciousness of the Backward and lower castes. For example, the Dalit Panthers (DP) developed some influence in Dalit Politics in Maharashtra. DP was inspired and borrowed their name from the Black Panther Party in the USA,[160]

Dalits declared 'we want to rule over the entire country.'[161] 'Our resolution will flash like lightening.'[162] To begin with, the Dalit youths articulated their unrest and resentment initially through literature.[163]

Raja Dhale's article 'Kala Swantantriya Din', i.e. Black Independence Day, published in August 1972 became controversial and created a sensation among the Dalits. With this, the term 'Dalit' came into vogue. Open confrontation between Dalit Panthers and upper-caste Hindus took place several times in the 1970s. The Worli riots of 1974 and Aurangabad riots of 1978 are well known.[164]

Dalit began to mirror shifting perspectives. Namdev Dhasal, the well known Marathi poet and activist of the Dalit Panther movement infused the term

> with a leftist vision to include not just the SCs but the economically oppressed classes within the ambit of the movement. For another Dalit activist from Maharashtra, Gangadhar Pantawane, the term Dalit did not refer only to a caste 'but was a symbol of change and revolution'.[165]

By 1972, the Dalit Panthers (DP) came into being as a distinctive cultural political group with their anchorage in urban Maharashtra, particularly in Bombay and Poona.[166] According to the DP, the Dalits were facing multiple problems like basic economic needs, social discrimination, political oppression and physical torture.[167] Dalits declared 'We want to rule over the entire country. Our target ... is not individual, but a whole system rotten to the core ...'.[168] Following the Panther, the Dalit movement throughout the country took on a multi-faceted expression.[169]

According to Gail Omvedt:

> The Dalit upsurge then found varying issues: the desire for recognition on human beings, the urge for education and a share in development, and the aspiration to political power. It took varying forms: efforts to gain power through the gun, through the schools, through the ballot, through marches in the streets and rallies and meetings in slums and villages, everywhere ....[170]

It is significant to note here that DP counted not only SCs and tribes and new Buddhists as Dalits but 'all SCs and tribes, landless laborers, small farmers and nomadic tribes that are committed to fighting injustice – stemming from political power, property, religious and social status'.[171]

The Dalit Sahitya emerged as a powerful expression of the subtle exploitative relations that prevailed in the urban and rural areas of Maharashtra including Marathwada.[172] The commonly shared pain spurred them to unite.[173]

They asserted that their fight was against 'Dalitva' that is socially untouchable status by birth.[174] To be a Dalit, they believed was no more a 'shameful' matter.[175] The main aim of the DP movement was for Dalits to have their fair share and voice in politics, development, education and attainment of equal rights. But DP was a short-lived movement and it eventually suffered from the same problems as the RPI.

One of the major reasons for the failure of the DP was that some of the leaders were co-opted to join the Congress. By including these leaders from the DP the party was able to woo the Dalit voters. In this way, the Congress became very influential for Dalit Consciousness (DC).

During this same period (late 1960s and 1970s), the Congress party tried to create a new socio-political support base for itself. It included poor, landless, and also Dalits (Harijan) and the Muslim minority. This was done mainly to woo Dalit voters. By appeasing this class the Congress party made some difference in its approach and orientation. By attracting this class, the party included some Dalit leaders in its wing. This also explains the *politicization* of castes in India. In order to give its due representation to Dalits, under the Indian Constitution, under Articles 330 and 332, seats are reserved for Dalits (SCs) in Lok Sabha (the lower house of Indian Parliament) and State Assemblies. Though the reservations were only for 10 years initially, they have been extended from time to time and exist until now. As Indian society is based on caste stratification, this has had a direct impact on voting patterns. Higher castes people had dominated politics in the past. However, with the advent of the green revolution, the backward castes became politically strong.

In addition to the reservation of seats in parliament, several welfare schemes were also initiated, which led to changes in the psyche of the Dalits. Most of the Dalits that Congress Party were attracting were poor and landless farmers. For this reason, the *Garibi Hatao* (a Hindi word that means 'eradicate poverty') and a 20-Point Programme were introduced. Other welfare schemes included digging of wells for making drinking water available, the redistribution of surplus land and the nationalization of banks so that small farmers could get credit and the landless Dalits could be employed (for details see, A.M. Zaidi [1986] as quoted in Ghanshyam Shah (ed.), *Dalit Identity and Politics* [2001], pp. 266–267).

Despite these reforms, Dalits – within the Congress – realized that they had little political power. Congress did try to make some welfare schemes exclusively for Dalits, but since the latter were not given any important political portfolios they felt they were being used only for the vote bank. As a result, Dalits felt not only politically discriminated but also alienated.

Although many felt alienated, there were some important politicians in Congress who arose from the Scheduled Castes. One was Jagjivan Ram, who succeeded in 'becoming a genuinely national figure through Congress'. Another was Bhole Paswan Shastri, who held the position of Chief Minister thrice.

Thus, there was some headway made, but it remained an important realization that the ideological and social make-up of Congress made it less welcoming to highly assertive advocates of the untouchable cause.

Oliver Mendelson quotes Atul Kohli to say that the Congress and Communist Party dominated governments in West Bengal have had a strikingly skewed caste composition.[176] This can be crystalised by reference to Ambedkar's description of Indian Communists as 'a bunch of Brahman boys'.[177]

It would be pertinent to note here that while the untouchables were a crucial Congress vote bank[178] in India as a whole and in a majority of individual states, even before the recent flux they did not cling to Congress in regions where another party or movement rose to dominance.[179] It will be recalled that in the era when they voted overwhelmingly for Congress their political and social power was considerably less than it is today.[180] A review of the history of Dalit Movement (attempted in the preceding pages) indicates that one of its consequences was the growth of Dalit Consciousness.[181] It may be relevant to examine here how this consciousness evolved during the pre and post-colonial period and what were the factors that caused their collective revolt in the past and present times. An attempt has also been made here to essay how the consciousness developed in the context of growth of their intellectual faculties and the emergence of the idea of a welfare state.

To trace the crystalisation of Dalit Consciousness, it is necessary here to recall the significant protest movements in India.[182] The Dalit Movement (DM) was, by and large, the result of the growth of Dalit Consciousness (DC) from the pre- to post-colonial era through political organization. At the same time, DC found its intellectual foundation in Dalit Intellectual Activity (DIC) with writers like Kabir, whom Ravidas, the Mahars of Lohari Khurd, used to recite.

Some other important writers who helped shape DC were Tukaram, Nandnar, Chokamela, Lok Kavi Behari Lal Harit, Mahatma Bakshidas, Swami Shankarnand, Ayodhyanath Brahmachari, Gopal Baba Valankar, Shivaram Jave Kamble, Kishan Fagu Bansode, Ambedkar, Namdev Dhasal, Harish Bansode. J.V. Pawar, Raja Dhale, U.N. Biswas, S. Biswas, Ranjeet Sikdar, Bimil Sarkar and L.R. Balley.

Dalit Consciousness in the pre- and post-1947 period also finds expression in the form of Dalit literature.[183] It implies how the Dalits feeling of exploitation has been expressed in various forms such as poetry, plays, essays and books.[184] These authors were mainly Dalits though a few non-Dalits too joined in protesting against their exploitation and in post-independence period some foreigners[185] also figured on the list. To trace the roots of this protest in Hindi literature, one has to go back to early medieval period. The couplets of Kabir and Ravidas provide ample evidence of contemporaneous disapproval of social inequalities.[186]

The linkage between the Dalit cultural tradition and the teachings of Kabir is evident in his *doha* (verse) that the Mahars of Lohari Khurd used to recite in Dalit locality.[187]

Similarly the Mahars of this region also integrated into their cultural consciousness and activism the form of 'abhanga' (a kind form of poetry from The Saint Tradition) and its content from the Nirankari tradition led by Tukaram, the revolutionary saint from medieval Maharashtra.[188] The abhanga runs as below:

> Ninda kache ghar Asare Sijari Nirmal Jahali Dehachi Pasali.[189]

Other contemporary authors include Nandnar and Chokhamela.[190]

We find some journals like *Adi-Hindu* and *Harijan*.[191] Other major works by Lok Kavi Beharilal Harit was *Achhuton Ka Betaj Badshah*, *Bihmayan* and *Jagjivan Jyoti*.[192] Some of the popular Dalit poets include Mahatma Bakshidas, Swami

Shankarnand and Ayhodhyanath Brahmachari who have put their stamp on Dalit intellectual map.[193]

The Maharashtra region which gave momentum to the Depressed Classes Movement, inspired writings all over the country.[194] The first Marathi Dalit journalist was Gopal Baba Valankar[195] followed by Shivaram Java Kamble[196], Kishan Fagn Bansode[197], Ambedkar[198] and many others.[199]

As Gopal Guru observes:

> The most authentic and vibrant cultural movement began to decline from 1969. This can be explained in terms of the following factors:
>
> The political subordination of the Dalit panthers to Congress party in Maharashtra also shows the corresponding subordination of the Dalit cultural movement in this region.[200]

It is historically true that Dalit women from different parts of Maharashtra did participate in Ambedkar's movement.[201] Ori was used as a very effective cultural idiom to create and conserve the critical energies among Dalit men and women.[202]

May Dari Nib! Nibale Phullera
Baba Sahebanchy Kotale Sonyehi Zalar![203]

Sonaychi Anghthi! Chandicha
Mndarka Babasahebauchy Bohat!

Bammin Ghat Kela vish Pajale Takat.[204]
Dilli Sharat Haldi Kunkwachi More!

Him Navardeo Bhata Bamnachya Ghari[205]

Thus the above Dalit feminist cultural intervention definitely indicates the cultural assertion of Dalit women in the social struggle against Brahmanical social order and the state.[206]

Dalit poetry frequently uses the sun as the metaphor for the movement led by Dr B.R. Ambedkar, often seeing him as the sun and the bringer of a totally new world.[207] À la:

The Sun of self-respect has burst into flame
Let it burn up these castes
Smash, break, destroy
These walls of hatred
Crush to Smithereens this eons-old

School of blindness
Rise, O people![208]

– After a 1000 years we are blessed
with a sunflower-giving –
now, now we must, take sunflowers,
turn, our faces to the Sun[209]

In this context, the post-Ambedkar Dalit movement has prescribed a revolutionary practice.[210] Also pertinent to mention here is the fact that there were years when the pages of *Janata*, Ambedkar's weekly were filled with reports of the struggles of workers and peasants against 'capitalists and landlords' as well as the fight of Dalits against atrocities.[211] In Ambedkar's words: 'Society has been aiming to lay a new foundation as was summarized by the French Revolution in three words: Fraternity, Liberty and Equality – it seems that the three can coexist only if one follows the way of the Buddha.'[212]

Militancy among Buddhists to fight for their just place in society has increased. The vocal section feels that they have found the new path – the path to attain equality.[213]

Harish Bansode expresses his agony, anger and hope in his poem 'Tumhi Bambla Aata':

– You were in the temple, we were on the steps;
Because you thought us untouchable.
But those days are over.[214]

It may be pertinent to note here that Dalit Literature Conference was called by Buddhist writers in 1959.[215] And after ten years *Asmitadarsh*[216], a journal devoted to Dalit literature was launched in 1969. Two Dalit writers – activists, Namdev Dhasal and J.V. Pawar, took the initiative in forming the Dalit Panthers in Bombay in 1972.[217] Another activist, Raja Dhale's article 'Kala Swatantra Divas', i.e. 'Black Independence Day', published in August 1972, became controversial.[218]

Gopal Guru observes:

> 'It is true that the cultural tradition of the Dalits in Maharashtra did not receive due recognition from the Maharashtrian upper caste society. In fact, on certain occasion, it was really run down by them. In this background, the emergence of the Dalit cultural movement in Maharashtra is a welcome development in as much

as it acquired for itself a distinct place in the cultural life of the state.'[219] The Dalit cultural and literary movements in addition to the above factors, also played an important role in creating and conserving the cultural political energies that were necessary for taking on the forces of hegemony and domination.[220]

In the other words of Sheoraj Bechain:

> In Gujarat, Gandhism hampered the growth of Dalit consciousness. The only interesting development was the launch of a magazine, *Dalit Panthers*, by Ramesh Chandra Parmar.[221]

The Karnataka literary movement, under the banner of Dalit Sangharsh Samiti, gave an impetus to their cause.[222] *Bheem Vani* is a prominent Kannada magazine.[223]

Sudha Pai observes about Tamil Nadu:

> Due to the Bhakti tradition, the dalit literature of the colonial period and dravadianism, particularly the mass movement led by Periyar, dalit consciousness in this region, compared to many parts of the sub-continent is rooted in the cultural moorings leading to deeper consciousness of identity.[224]

Dalit Consciousness and action in Tamil Nadu can be distinguished from the two other 'models' on the sub-continent in the colonial period: the Gandhian and the Ambedkarite.[225] As a result in the post-independence period, the Dalits in Tamil Nadu initially supported mainstream parties, such as the DMK and the Congress. This was despite the fact of caste clashes between them and the non-Brahmans 1940s onwards, due to their differing class interests.[226] It is only from the 1980s that the DM in the state has intensified due to the larger process of democratization since independence.[227]

However, they have failed to create a 'wider Dalit indentity' mobilising all the exploited and oppressed on a common platform of Dalit-Shudra in Tamil Nadu.'[228]

Regarding the state of Uttar Pradesh, Sudha Pai opines: 'In contrast to parts of western India which came under the influence of Babasaheb Ambedkar, UP did not experience any large-scale anti-caste movement during the colonial period which resulted in delayed development of political consciousness among SCs.'[229]

The period between 1940s and 70s only saw the formation and decline of RPI activity followed by the formation of BKD.[230] It was only in the 1980s, that the SC movement shifted its preference to the banner of the BSP.[231]

In Bengal today, one comes across the writings of U.N. Biswas, S. Biswas, Ranjeet Sikdar and Bimil Sarkar.[232]

In Punjab, L.R. Balley took the lead in the Dalit field.[233] Despite the fact the Panjab Government banned his works; *Hinduism Dharam Ya Kalank*; went into its fifth edition, shows the growing intolerance among upper castes.[234]

The following contemporary writings/ poems on the condition of Dalits reveal that their condition has still not fully improved.[235] They were still denied their social economic and political rights.[236]

Some of the excerpts from poems are as follows:

> 'Chashme hakikat ko Dekho
> Udhar Nahin Idhar Hoon Yaron
>
> Dhoondo Mat Verrane Mein;'[237]
>
> 'Ek Dalit Makaan Banata Hai
> Majdoori Karta Hai
> Hindustan Ki Swarna Jatiyan,
>
> Is Prakar ke Karya Karne walon ko
> Ghrana ke Drshti Se Dekhti Hein';[238]
>
> 'Yug Badla Shasan Badla
> Tasveer Na Badli Daliton Ki';[239]
>
> 'Bundele Harbole ne, Ghad De Thi Jhoothi Kahani Ko!
> Jalkari Ran Mein Jhooji Par Gaya Laxmi Rani Ko'[240]

It may be noted that the aim of all those involved in the intellectual activity has been to sensitize the Dalit masses to work for their own social, cultural and political upliftment.[241] Today we find in booklets not the history of Dalits but history written by Dalits.[242] It is different from the Dalit History written during the Dalit movement in Maharashtra in the 1960s.[243]

It is interesting to note that the folk symbols a discussion strategy has been used by the Bahujan Samaj Party (BSP) in the construction of its political language. Its political discourse includes Ravidas (Rabidas), Kabir, Jhalkaribai, Phule, Periyar and Ambedkar among others.

Thus the Dalit intellectual activists in contemporary India represents a very interesting scenario in which an urgent need is felt to make theoretical sense of the Dalit reality.

In fact, the encounter with modernity of groups such as the Dalits could not be explained within the terms of a global narrative about the fate of modernity. There should be a cultural theory of modernity which could allow us to see modernity as a multilinear and layered processes of historical transformation.

This discussion of the DM and DC would be incomplete without the mention of job reservation and vote bank politics in India. For example, was there any simultaneous positive impact of DM, DC or DIC on the Backward Caste politics in India. If so, how?

The irony is that reservation of jobs for the amelioration of the BCs and the SCs had, initially, been conceived with the solemn intention of improving the lot of the downtrodden. As of late, however, job reservation has been reduced to being a bait to lure the gullible and set at naught all the gains from this well-intentioned movement of our forefathers. It is a big bait in the sense that it is an effective tool in the hands of greedy politicians to catch the votes of the BCs, which are 40 per cent plus of India's population. So the promise of reservation lures in voters (thus, becoming a big 'vote bank') by giving the BCs the allurement of reservation in studies vocation. It has worked wonders at times. Unfortunately, the reservation of jobs for few BCs has resulted in more and more people from other castes blocking railway tracks, roads, transport, and paralyzing government machinery. Today, reservation has come to assume such divergent and gigantic proportions that it threatens to turn the applecart of sanity upside down. Every new dawn brings to the fore fresh demands for reservations from diverse quarters.

The promise of job reservation also suffers from inefficient implementation. Despite all the efforts on the part of the governments of the day, the benefits of reservation could not percolate down to the different sections of the SCs in an equitable manner. In so many odd years of the reservation process, only a small fraction of the SC and BC population has benefitted. The root cause of the malaise is the lack of education. The government has, from time to time, introduced schemes to educate the so-called backwards or SCs. For example, Sarv Shiksha Abhiyan (English translation: Education-for-All Movement) is an Indian government programme aimed at universalization of elementary education 'in a time-bound manner'. According to the 86th Amendment of the Indian Constitution, it makes education free and compulsory for children from the age of six to fourteen. It has also been added in the list of fundamental rights for Indian citizens, but, sadly, these initiatives have an unfailing streak of failure. Most of the Extremely Backward Classes (EBCs) have an age-old belief that the greater the number of earning hands, the better the quality of life. That has resulted in population explosion, illiteracy, landlessness, child marriage, hooliganism and so on. All this has ominously combined to retard the progress of the SCs to quite an extent. As debated frequently, it is obvious that there are vested interests at work and no genuine concern for the empowerment of the SCs and other BCs is evident.

So, at one level, political measures for job reservation have had little practical impact for many of the SCs. However, there has been quite a discernible change in the general approach to the SCs. They are, no more, looked down upon as lesser mortals by the upper castes. The changing of the guard, at all levels of society, with a much younger crop of citizen taking over the reins, has erased caste considerations to a great extent from our dealings, actions, and interactions with this special segment which, earlier, was fully subservient to the upper castes.

Vote bank politics continues to play havoc with the body politic of a very big section of the underprivileged sections of Indian society. For example, as per the 2011 Census, Dalits comprised one-third of Punjab's population of 27 million. However, the Dalits are still split between the *Adhidharmi* (a Ravidassia community of Punjab) and the *Valmiki/Mazhabi* people, and these two communities have not been politically aligned. The latter have steered clear of the BSP, whose politics veers around Dalit issues. The schism between the Adidharmis/Ramdassias and the Valmikis/Majhabis remains wide despite the efforts of Kanshi Ram, the proponent of Dalit political consciousness and founder of the Bahujan Samaj Party. Though he influenced the politics of India, Kanshi could not convince Adidharmis/Ramdassias and Valmikis/Majhabis to stay under one roof for assertion of their political and democratic rights. BSP has, largely, remained a party of the Adidharmi/Ravidassia community in Punjab. The social engineering formula, which envisaged bringing upper castes closer to BSP, could not bring together even the two Dalit communities of the state. The first split in the party happened on caste lines in the early 1990s as the Valmiki community leader, Ravi Das Nahar, parted ways with the BSP (Ambedkar). At the same time, families of Dalit leaders continued their dominance in the Congress party and Kanshi Ram painstakingly groomed young leaders.

In recent years, the BJP has promoted Adidharmi/Ravidassia community leaders who are already divided among Congress and BSP in order to increase their support. The BJP has been trying to wean these sections away from the Congress and has had some success. The BJP has now come to power in the 2014 Parliamentary Elections and is also ruling in more than half the states of the country

During the last few years, the Shiromani Akali Dal–SAD (Badal) party has desperately wooed the Adidharmi and Ramdassia by promoting a few faces from the community, while most other leaders, including Rajesh Bagha, Chairman, Punjab Commission for Scheduled Castes, Punjab, are from Adidharmi/Ramdassia community with the sole exception of Chunnilal Bhagat.

The tensions between the Adhidharmi and Valmiki communities continue to be evident. In the 2014 Parliamentary Elections, Hans Raj Hans, who is from the Valmiki community, led a tirade against Tinu of the SAD who is an Adidharmi. Tinu lost the election to Chaudhary Santokh Singh of the Congress when Dalit votes got divided. Valmikis have been demanding 12.5 per cent reservation of jobs and studies/admissions to state run educational institutes. Admissions for schools means that entrance would not be based on merit but instead would accommodate students with much lesser marks in qualifying exams. These demands have been vehemently opposed by the Adidharmis. This latest development in Punjab throws ample light on the decisive role that SCs and BCs can now afford to play in their backyards.[244]

The result of the political climate and the division between the Adidharmis and Valmikis is that ambition and vested interests have derailed the progress of the SCs and other Dalits. The rewards are covered and snatched away in due course. Their ever burgeoning numbers make them attractive for political power, but splinter groups among them make the waters dirtier and murkier. Congress has some leaders whose familial domination continues. BSP founder, Kanshi Ram, made leaders out of common workers while in the last few years SAD has been promoting leaders who were earlier part of BSP. With an eye on the vote bank, the upper caste dominated BJP has started patronizing SC leaders. The BJP is seen to be making very strong attempts after its victory in the recently held parliamentary polls in Haryana and Maharashtra to woo the SCs and their tribes.

Schism between the two largest communities of Punjab remained wide even though the proponent of dalit political consciousness and founder of the Bahujan Samaj Party, Kanshi Ram could not bring the two together. Though he influenced the politics of India and damaged the Congress Party permanently with his politics, Kanshi could not convince Adidharmis/Ramdassias and Valmiki/Mazhabis to stay under one roof for assertion of their political and democratic rights. BSP has, largely, remained a party of Adidharmis/Ramdassias community in Punjab. The social engineering formula, which envisaged bringing upper castes closer, could not bring together even the two dalit communities of the state. The first split in the party happened on caste lines in the early 1990s as Valmiki community leader, Ravi Das Nahar parted ways with the BSP (Ambedkar)s while families of dalit leader continue their dominance in the Congress party. Kanshi Ram, painstakingly, groomed young leaders.

With Mayawati having her own way of managing the party affairs, BSP's graph shows a perceptible downward spiral and so many leaders parted ways. BJP is perceived to be a party dominated by upper caste Hindus, but of late, keeping in mind the vote bank, they have started partonizing and promoting SC leaders. The provision for reserved constituencies has, to a large extent, lent fillip to the ambition of the enterprising among the SCs to scale newer heights.

According to Sudhir Sharma:

> A cursory perusal of the scenario is enough to conclude that from being just the groundlings who depended entirely on the goodwill of the upper castes, the SCs have travelled the forbidden path and straddled across many an impediment and carved a niche for themselves in the body politic of the country after a sustained campaign which had early tidings in the foresight and vision of stalwarts like Mahatma Gandhi and B.R. Ambedkar whose genuine concern for this centuries old problem of deprivation, exploitation and discrimination meted out to almost 50 per cent of the country's population for no fault of its own, has already pulled the SCs out of the morass of ambiguity, hate and malice. Grant of reservation in multifarious ways has gone a long way in, partially, healing the wounds inflicted since times immemorial but stretching the reservation issue too far is having adverse effect on the psyche of the youth from the other sections and some remedial measures are sought to be applied, and justifiably too. Quest for reservation by various sections of people is likely to bring people on the brink and already, there is open resentment against reservation.

Reservation continues to be a source of strife. Just recently (14 November 2014), the Bombay High Court stayed 16 per cent reservation for Marathas in jobs and education that had been introduced that year by faulting the data used by the state to back the assertion that the community is backward. The court also put on hold the 5 per cent quota in public employment under a special BC category to 50 subcastes among Muslims. If some sort of sanity is not sought to be incorporated in the dealings with the SCs, a cursory glance at the entire gamut of things as they have been is enough to set the alarm bells ringing.

The ever burgeoning lust for reservation and its inherent advantages among the SCs is not going to beget the desired result and all the good that has filtered down is likely to beat a retreat if some sort of restraint is not exercised. The greed that stretches the reservation chord is likely to snap it beyond repair as mistrust and simmering resentment could set the clock back and result in bad blood and chaos between the castes that has been hitherto incomprehensible.

The Dalit intellectual activists[245] tried to answer: How the Dalits acted in the past? What was the ideological base for their action? Or why is it important to construct a Dalit epistemology?

The caste system and its social stratification as understood by upper castes exists both in unwritten and written forms. In response, these activists did express various insults and discriminations faced by Dalits in various articles and the related literature but no theory on Dalit or *Dalan* has been made so far. An attempt is made in the next two chapters in this direction.

Notes

1. Dhanajay Keer (1962). *Dr. Ambedkar: Life and Mission.* Bombay: Popular. p. 382. Also see Oliver Mendelson and Marika Vicziany (2000). *The Untouchables.* Delhi: Cambridge University Press. p. 22. Also *Dharamshastras of Gotham* – Wikipedia, the free encyclopedia.
2. Uday Mehta (1998). 'Untouchability and Social Transformation in India'. *One India One People.* October, p. 17. Also Patrick Olivelle (2004). *The Law Code of Manu.* New York: OUP.
3. Ramashray Roy and V.B. Singh (1987). *Between Two Worlds: A Study of Harijan Elites.* Delhi: Discovery. p. 1. Also see 'In Ambedkar's Country, D still can enter Temples'. (2000). *The Hindustan Times.* April 14. Also *Introduction to Apastamba* (Hindu Scriptures Website).
4. Koenaad (1993). *Dr. Ambedar: A True Aryan.* Delhi: Voice of India. p. 38.
5. Nicolas B. Dirks (2001). *Castes of Mind.* Princeton, NJ: Princeton University Press. p. 3. Also MSS Pandhian (2002). 'One Step Outside Modernity'. *Economic and Political Weekly.* Vol. XXXVII, no. 18, May 4–10. pp. 1735–36.
6. Sukhadeo Throat (2002). 'Oppression and Denial'. *Economic and Political Weekly.* Vol. XXXVII, no. 6, February 9, p. 572.
7. Ibid.
8. Nicholas B. Dirks (2001). *Castes of Mind.* (Princeton, NJ: Princeton University Press). p. 3.
9. Quoted in M.S.S. Pandhian (2002). 'One Step Outside Modernity'. *Economic and Political Weekly.* Vol. XXXVII, no. 18, May 4–10, pp. 1735–36.

10. Gail Omvedt (1999). 'Dalits and Elections–I', *The Hindu*. November 5.
11. Ibid. Their (voter) turnout has been higher, according to surveys conducted by the Centre for the Study of Developing Societies (CSDS) in Delhi.
12. Aditya Nigam (2002). 'In Search of a Bourgeoisie', *Economic and Political Weekly*. Vol. XXXVII, no. 13, March 30, pp. 1190–93.
13. See Sukhadeo Thorat (2002). 'Oppression and Denial'. *Economic and Political Weekly*. Vol. XXXVII, no. 6, February 9, p. 572.
14. Ibid., p. 578.
15. Susmita Dasgupta (2001). 'The Politics of Mobilisation of the Backward Classes – Malaise, Diagnosis and Treatment'. Summary of paper presented at a seminar. Pune University. p. 19.
16. Gail Omvedt (2002). 'Udaarikaran Se Hogi Daliton Ki Mukti'. *Rashtriya Sahara*. January 26, Hastshep, p. 2 (in Hindi).
17. Rashtriya Sahara (2002). Hastshep, January 26, p. 2 (Hindi).
18. Ramashray Roy and V.B. Singh, no. 3 , p. 103, 118.
19. This is accompanied by ghettoes and semi-ghettoes.
20. P.R. Ram (1998). 'Purity, Pollution and Quest for Social Justice'. *One India One People*. Vol. 2/3. October, p. 8.
21. Devabrata Bose (1968). *The Problems of Indian Society* Bombay: Popular. p. 253.
22. 'The Problem' (1998). *Seminar* 471. pp. 12–13.
23. See op. cit, n. 3, p. 1.
24. A.K. Deshi and H. Singh (1995), 'Education, Labour Market Distortions and Relative Earning of Different Religious – Caste Categories in India. *Canadian Journal of Development Studies*. December 21.
25. For details see, R.C. Yadav and Rajbir Singh (1994). *India's Unequal Citizens*. Delhi: Manohar. p. 45.
26. Manusmriti. 8.417
27. Ibid., 4.78–81.
28. Vashisthadharmasutra. 18. 11–15
29. R.C. Yadav and Rajbir Singh. op. cit., no. 25. p. 45.
30. W. E. S. Dubois (1918). *Black Folk, Then and Now*. New York: Albany. pp. 75–80.

31. The perpetrators almost always belong to the upper castes, who know that the political system in their monopoly that they will get away with almost any outrage.
32. Ibid. À la Karnataka, Andhra, Orissa and Gujarat.
33. 'Challenging Untouchability: Dalit Initiative and Experience in Karnataka'. (1998). *The Statesman*. November 2.
34. More than 70 per cent of rural Dalits are landless labourers, most of them are indebted to the blood-sucking money-lenders. (Ram, P.R. (1998). 'Purity, Pollution and Quest for Social Justice'. *One India One People*. Vol.2/3, October, p. 9).
35. The dispute remained unsolved till the collector advised to use dispensable cups in the area (Rahman, Syed Ubaidur (1998). 'Social Tensions in the Indian Society'. *One India One People*. Vol. 2/3. October. p. 14).
36. They are required to push their bikes through the village and ride only after reaching the outskirts.
37. During Vinayaka (Ganapati) festival, the pujari told me to (Ellapa) 'Leave ₹ 2 on the floor. I can't take it in my hand'. Do you know the solution our MLA came up with? He said, 'Why not have separate tea shops for different castes?' Sainath P. (1998). 'Glass Struggle Continues'. *The Hindu*. Sunday Magazine. November 15. p. II.
38. Sadanand A. Shetty (1998). 'It is a national shame'. *One India One People*. Vol. 2/3, October, Editorial page.
39. 'In Ambedkar's country, D Still Can't Enter Temples'. (2000). *The Hindustan Times*. April 14. Dalits here remember Swami Agniwesh's padyatra from Udaipur to Nathdwara temple in the eighties, when despite days of tension and a national outcry, he was not allowed to enter the temple with Dalits.
40. Ibid.
41. But there is a rare exception – an aberration. A 55 year old Vonguri Muttaiah is like any other temple priest. The difference is that this priest, who presides the Ram temple at Vallabhi village in Khamman district happens to be a Harijan.
42. In a spine-chilling crime in Lalitpur, a 13-month baby was thrown into a burning furnace by a brick-kiln owner, while in Pratapgarh, six Dalit children were forced to dip their hands into a cauldron of boiling oil. 'Be A Child or Dalit Not Both'. (1999). *The Pioneer*. April 14. p. 1. Also see, 'Mayawati plays sister to Jehrana's Dalit'. (2002). *Indian Express*. June 16.

43. T.K. Raja Lakshmi (2001). 'Castes and Killings'. *Frontline*. July 20. p. 38.
44. Arun Kumar Tripathi (2001). 'Dalit Digvijay Aur Agneda'. *Rashtriya Sahara*. August 11, Hastshep, p. 2. (Hindi).
45. 'Treat Caste on a par with racism apartheid'. (2000). *The Hindu*. April 20.
46. Ghanshyam Shah (ed.) (2001). *Dalit Identity and Politics*. New Delhi: Sage. p. 37.
47. Ghanshyam Shah (2001). 'Dalit Movements and the Search for Identity' in Ghanshyam Shah (ed.), *Dalit Identity and Politics*. Delhi: Sage. p. 37.
48. M.N. Srinivas (1997). 'Varna and caste' in Dipankar Gupta (ed.), *Social Stratification*. Delhi: Oxford University Press. p. 28.
49. R.C. Yadav and Rajbir Singh (1994). op. cit. no. 25, p. 46.
50. Sudha Pai (2002). *Dalit Assertion and the Unfinished Democratic Revolution*. Delhi: Sage. Editor's Note.
51. Koenadd (1993). op. cit. no. 4. p. 38.
52. Nandu Ram (1995). *Beyond Ambedkar*. Delhi: Har Anand. p. 55.
53. Chitra Tiwari (1963). *Sudras in Manu*. Delhi: Moti Lal Banarsi Dass. p. 15.
54. Kancha Ilaiah (2001). 'Dalitism versus Brahminism: The Epistemological conflict in History', in Ghanshyam Shah (ed.), *Dalit Identity and Politics*. New Delhi: Sage. 21.
55. Kancha Ilaiah (1991). 'Gautam Budha as a Political Philosopher'. Ph.D. Thesis, Chapter 4. Department of Political Science, Osmania University. Hyderabad. Also Basanta Kumar Mallik (1988). 'Marx and Ambedkar: A Comparative Study', *Mainstream*. Vol. XXVI, no. 28, April 23. Also B.R. Ambedkar (1987). *Writings and Speeches*. Bombay: Education Department, Government of Maharashtra. Vol. III. pp. 443–44.
56. The Nanda emperors of Maghda were Shudras, there is every reason to believe that the Mauryan and Gupta emperors were also Shudras G.K. Pillai (1959). *Origin and Development of Caste*. Delhi: Kitab Mahal. p. 11.
57. This at once sounds like the justification par excellence for social division for varna though not for jati. The year is ordered by division of seasons (Ritu) with their own typical

outlook and characteristic activities, and similarly society should be divided in classes with their own duties and destructive customs. Koenaad Elst (1993). op. cit. no. 4. p. 46.

58. At the worldly level, truthfulness implies being true to one's inner qualities to ones vocation. As there are human beings of different qualities (gunas, symbolically corresponding to 'colours', varnas) so there are different social roles to be filled by people with appropriate vocation.
59. One's own duty.
60. At any rate the term Swadharma can perfectly be interpreted as meaning 'duty grounded in one's natural quality' rather than 'hereditary duty'.
61. These broken men were then allowed to live alongwith other communities, but on the outside.
62. Which was written during 1200 B.C. to 1000 B.C. So in the early vedic times, it is said that all were equals and there was no trace of untouchability as we see today. R.B. Tripathi (1994). *Dalits: A Sub-Human Society*. Delhi: Ashish. p.2.
63. They were converted by the Aryan invaders who used caste as a political and social instrument of subjugation into lowly servants and untouchables. Sudha Pai (2002). *Dalit Assertion and the Unfinished Democratic Revolution*. New Delhi: Sage. p. 48.
64. If it was so then, what was the meaning of the Rigvedic injunction Krinvanto Vishwmaryam? (Make the entire world Arya). Could they change the converts' colour also?. R.C. Yadav and Rajbir Singh. (1994). R.C. Yadav and Rajbir Singh. op. cit. no. 25. p. 42.
65. Ramahray Roy and V.B. Singh (1987). op. cit. no. 3, p. 81. Also H. Kotani (ed.). (1997). *Caste System: Untouchability and the Depressed*. Delhi: Manohar. p. 10.
66. Mayawati Advocate (2000). *Bahujan Samaj Aur Uski Rajneeti*. Delhi: Bahujan Samaj Party Publishers. p. 1.
67. See, Gail Omvedt as quoted in Uday Mehta (1998). 'Untouchables and Social Transformation in India'. *One India One People*. Vol. 2/3, October, p. 17. Also R.C.Yadav and Rajbir Singh. op. cit. no. 25, p. 42. Also Gail Omvedt (1999). 'The Dravidian Movement–II'. *The Hindu*. June 22.
68. Purnendu S. Kavoori (2002). 'The Varna Trophic System'. *Economic and Political Weekly*, Vol. XXXVII, no. 12, March 23–29, p. 1156.

69. Ranganata R. Diwaka (ed.) (1968). *Karnataka through the Ages*. Mysore: Government of Karnataka Publication. pp. 414–449.
70. Pradeep Kumar (1999). 'BSP Breaking Ground Realities in Uttar Pradesh'. *Mainstream*. May 1. p. 18. Also see Narendra Kumar (2000). 'Dalit and Shudra Politics and Anti-Brahman Movement'. *Economic and Political Weekly*. Nov. 4. p. 3977.
71. Uday Mehta (1998). 'Untouchability and Social Transformation in India'. *One India One People*. October. p. 17.
72. Oliver Mendelson and Marika Vicziany (2000). *The Untouchables: Subordination, Poverty and the State in Modern India*. Delhi: Cambridge University Press, p. 22.
73. Linda Hess (1983). *The Bijak of Kabir*. San Francisco: North Point Press. p. 25.
74. Gopal Guru (2001). 'The Interface between Ambedkar and Dalit Cultural Movement in Mahrashtra' in Ghanshyam Shah (ed.) (2001). *Dalit Identity and Politics*. New Delhi: Sage. p. 166.
75. Ibid. p. 166.
76. Syed Ubaidur Rahman (1998). 'Social Tensions in the Indian Society'. *One India, One People*. October, p. 13.
77. Gopal Guru, op. cit. no. 74, p. 156.
78. Poet Chokha Mela was an untouchable Mahar. See S.P. Punalekar (2001). 'Dalit Literature and Dalit Identity'. In Ghanshyam Shah (ed.). op. cit. no. 74. n. 35. p. 216. Also see Eleanor Zelliot (2001). *From Untouchable to Dalit: Essays on Ambedkar's Movement*'. Delhi: Manohar. p. 270.
79. Jayashree Gokhale-Turner (1981). 'Bhakti or Vidroha: Continuity and Change in Dalit Sahitya'. In Jayant Lele (ed.). *Tradition and Modernity in Bhakti Movement*. Leiden: E.J. Brill. p. 32.
80. Oliver Mendelson and Marika Vicziany. op. cit. no. 72. p. 24.
81. P.G. Friedlander (1987). 'An Introduction to Ravidas'. SOAS Seminar. December. Also see David Lorenzen (1981). 'The Kabir Panth Heretics to Hindus' in D.N. Lorenzen (ed.). *Religious Change and Cultural Domination*. Mexico City: El Colegio de Mexico. pp. 151–171.
82. Chandra Bhan Prasad and Sheoraj Singh Bechain (2000). 'Where Non-Dalits Commentators Err'. *The Hindu*. January 4, p. 21. (Book Review).

83. Oliver Mendelson and Marika Vicziany. op. cit. no. 72. p. 26.
84. The Brahman sepoy's objection was the khalasi asking for the drinking vessel would pollute his mouth. He had been biting off the caps of gun cartridges sealed with animal fat. Also see. Trilok Nath (1987). *Politics of Depressed Classes.* Delhi: Deputy. p. 24.
85. Eleanor Zelliot (2001). 'Dalit Trends and Dalit Consciousness' in Nirja Gopal Jayal and Sudha Pai (ed.). *Democratic Governance in India*. New Delhi. Sage. p. 236. Also Irawati Karve (1988). 'On the Road: A Maharashtrian Pilgrimage' in Eleanor Zelliot and Maxine Bernsten (ed.). *The Experience of Hinduism: Essays on Religion in Maharashtra.* Albany: State University of New York Press. pp. 142–71. Also see Guy A. Deleury (1960). *The Cult of Vithoba.* Pune: Deccan College Postgraduate Research Institute. p. 61. Also Jayashree Gokhale (1993). *From Concessions to Confrontation: The Politics of an Indian Untouchability Community.* Bombay: Popular. p. 42. For further details see Juergensmeyer (1982). *Religion as a Social Vision: The Movement Against Untouchability in the 20th Century Punjab.* Berkeley: University of California Press. pp. 25–30.
86. Oliver Mendelson and Marika Vicziany (2000). op. cit. no. 72. p. 26.
87. Nandu Ram (1995). *Beyond Ambedkar.* Delhi: Har Anand. p. 62.
88. S.M. Gaikwad (1998). 'Ambedkar and Indian Nationalism'. *Mainstream*. Vol. XXXIII, no. 10, March 7, p. 515. Also Monu Nalapat (1998). 'Dalit vs the Rest'. *One India One People*. Vol. 2/3. p. 7.
89. B. Krishna Reddy (1995). 'Ambedkar and Dalits: An Anthropological Perspective' in V.T. Patel (ed.). *Studies in Ambedkar.* Delhi: Devika. p. 91.
90. Ibid.
91. Ghanshyam Shah's article (2001), *Dalit Identity and Poltics.* New Delhi: Sage. p. 210.
92. As an umbrella, it refers to backward and lower castes.
93. Kancha Ilaiah (2001). 'Dalitism versus Brahminism: The Epistemological conflict in History', in Ghanshyam Shah (ed.), *Dalit Identity and Politics.* New Delhi: Sage. p. 124.

94. Gail Omvedt (2001). 'Ambedkar and After: The Dalit Movement in India' in Ghanshyam Shah (ed.) (2001). *Dalit Identity and Politics*. New Delhi: Sage. p. 158.
95. op. cit. no. 93. p. 124.
96. Gopal Guru and V. Geetha (2000). 'New Phase of Dalit-Bahujan Activity'. *Economic and Political Weekly*. Vol.XXV, no. 3, January 15–21. pp. 130–134.
97. Gail Omvedt (1999). 'The Dravidian Movement–II'. *The Hindu*. June 22. Also see Syed Iqbal (1998). 'The Dalit Dilemma'. *One India One People*. p. 15.
98. Ibid. Also see op. cit. no. 72. p. 97.
99. Ibid.
100. Pradeep Kumar (1999).'BSP Breaking Ground Reality in Uttar Pradesh', *Mainstream.*, May 1, p. 18.
101. C.P. Bhambhri (1999). 'Dialectics of Caste and Casteism'. *Economic and Political Weekly*. Vol. XXXIV, no. 36. September 4. p. 2619.
102. Ibid.
103. Gail Omvedt (2000). 'The Purpose of Reservation–I'. *The Hindu*. March 24.
104. Ibid. Also P.R. Ram (1998). 'Purity, Pollution and Quest for Social Justice'. *One India One People*. October, p. 8.
105. Gail Omvedt (1999). The Dravidian Movement II. *The* Hindu, June 22, Also see Pradeep Kumar (1999). ' Dalits and the Bahujan Samaj Party in Uttar Pradesh: Issues and Challenges'. *Economic and Political Weekly*, April 3. p. 822.
106. V. Krishna Ananth (2000). 'Periyar – defied yet diluted'. *The Hindu*. October 1, p.19.
107. And how they, in the dominant nationalist thinking, remain as 'collaborators' with the British, would illustrate this. M.S.S. Pandhian (2002). 'One Step Outside Modernity'. *Economic and Political Weekly*. Vol. XXXVII, no. 18, May 4–10, p. 1737.
108. See op. cit. no. 105. p. 170.
109. See op. cit. no. 72. p. 97.
110. K. Saradmoni (1980). *Emergence of a Slave Caste: Pulayas of Kerala*. Delhi. People's Publishing House. p.135. Also see JFT Jordens (1987). *Dayanand Saraswati: His Life and Ideas*. Delhi: Oxford University Press. pp. 144–147.

111. At the time, when Phule was propounding his radical attack in Maharashtra.

112. Established in 1886.

113. Vithal Ramji Shinde established the Depressed Classes Mission in 1906 and started hostels and educational institutions for them. Bhauyrao Patel started a boarding school called Shahu Boarding for the Mahars of Satara. Gopalbaba Walangkar dedicated himself to the emancipation of Dalits followed by Shivram Janba Kamble. In Vidarbha, similar work was carried out by Kisan Fager Bandsode Ganesh Akkaji Gawai and Kalicharan Nand Gavali. We find a pre-Ambedkar Dalit leader, Kisan Faguji Bansode, a Mahar journalist of Nagpur, asking the 'Aryans' to stop torture of the oppressed people.

114. Rebati Ballav Tripathi (1994). *Dalits: A Sub-Human Society*. Delhi: Ashish. p. 23. The Congress did nothing .... It was a formal fulfillment of the conditions which the depressed classes had made for giving their support to the Congress League Scheme.

115. All of these caste-based movements were committed to the goals of ritual self-reform, education and gaining access to employment under the State.

116. Jayshree Gokhale (1993). *From Concessions to Confrontation. The Politics of An Indian Untouchabiliy Community*. Bombay: Popular. p. 3.

117. On 23 March, 1918.

118. Devbrata Bose (1968). *The Problems of Indian Society*. Bombay: Popular. p. 253.

119. Ranade as quoted in Gail Omvedt (1994). *Dalits and Democratic Revolution*. New Delhi: Sage. pp. 157–159, 250–255.

120. R.S. Khare (1984). *The Untouchables as Himself: Ideology, Identity and Pragmatism among the Lucknow Chamars*. Cambridge: Cambridge University Press. pp. 18–25.

121. B.R. Ambedkar (1948). *The Untouchables: Who were they and why they became Untouchables*. Delhi: Amrit. p.143.

122. M.S. Gore (1993). *The Social Context of an Ideology* (Ambedkar's Social Political Thought). Delhi. Sage. p. 74.

123. Basanta Kumar Mallik (1992). 'Ambedkar As a Builder of Modern India'. *Mainstream*. Vol. XXX. no. 25. April 11. pp. 21–25.

124. W.N. Kuber (1973). *Ambedkar: A Critical Study*. Delhi. India. p. 63. Also M.S. Gore (1993). *The Social Context of an Ideology: Political and Social Thought*. Delhi: Sage. p. 123.
125. Mahatma Gandhi (1934). *The Harijan*. April 20.
126. Mark Lindley (2004). Changes in Mahatma Gandhi's views on caste and inter marriage. Turkish University Academic Web Journal. .
127. For details see Radhika Ramaseshan (1995). 'Dalit Politics in Uttar Pradesh'. *Seminar–425*. January, p. 2612. Also Devbrata Bose (1968). *The Problems of Indian Society*. Bombay: Popular. p. 23. Also Raj Kumar (1996). 'Relevance of Ambedkarism in India'. *Mainstream*. Vol. XXXIV. no. 24. May 18. p. 24.
128. Nirmal Kumar (1992). 'Gandhi's Struggle Against Communalism and Casteism'. *Mainstream*. Vol. XXX. no. 51. October 10. p. 77. Also I.A. Ezekiel (1971). 'Ambedkar – the Social Revolutionary'. *Times Weekly*. April 11. p. 245. Also Eleanor Zelliot (1972). 'Gandhi and Ambedkar: A Study in Leadership' in Michael Mahar (ed.). *Untouchability in Contemporary India*. Tucson: University of Arizona Press. pp. 69, 72, 75.
129. B.R. Ambedkar (1979). Writings and Speeches. Bombay: Education Department. Government of Maharashtra. Vol. I. p. 41.
130. I.A. Ezekiel (1971). 'Ambedkar the Social Revolutionary'. *Times Weekly*. April 11. p. 250.
131. Vijay Prasad (1996). 'The Untouchable Question'. *Economic and Political Weekly*. March 2. pp. 554–556.
132. Awadhendra Sharan (2001). 'Colonialism and the Question of Untouchability', paper presented at a Seminar on 'Social Oppression and the Emancipatory Project' in Panjab University, Chandigarh. February 27–28.
133. Ibid. also Census of India (1871–72). General Report. pp. 22, 26.
134. Awadhendra Sharan (2001). 'Colonialism and the Question of Untouchability', paper presented at a Seminar on 'Social Oppression and the Emancipatory Project' in Panjab University, Chandigarh. February 27–28.
135. R.K. Kshirsagar (1994). *Dalit Movement in India and its Leaders*. Delhi: M.D Publications Pvt. Ltd.

136. Kagzi, Mangal Chander Jain (1976). *Segregation and Untouchability Abolition*. Delhi: Metropolitan. p. 218.
137. For details see Sudha Pai (2001). 'From Harijan to Dalits Identity Formation, Political Consciousness and Electoral Mobilization of the Scheduled Castes in Uttar Pradesh' in Ghanshyam Shah (ed.). *Dalit Identity and Politics*. New Delhi: Sage. p. 262. Also Sudha Pai (1998). 'The BSP in Uttar Pradesh'. *Seminar* 471. November. p. 38.
138. Desai (1985). *Caste, Conflict and Reservation*. Delhi: Eastern p. 119.
139. B.V. Bhosale (2001). *Issues of Mobilisation For Scheduled Castes in Maharashtra: A Case Study of Charmakars*. Paper present at Seminar. University of Pune. p.7. Also see Gail Omvedt (2001). op. cit. no. 94. p. 150.
140. The need of political alliance broke their unity and Congress in a clever manifestation of Dalit leadership, neutralised their movement and Dalit leaders were co-opted to such an extent that they lost their identity.
141. It prescribed more stringent punishment for those who practice untouchability, replacing the Untouchable Offence Act, 1955.
142. T.K. Oommen (1990). *Protest and Change: Studies in Social Movements*. New Delhi: Sage. p. 264.
143. It represented a coming together of socialists, communists and Dalits.
144. T.V. Rajeshwar (1998). 'The Curse of Caste System'. *The Hindustan Times*. November 22. p. 13.
145. For details see Girish Menon (2000). 'Creamy Layer Issue: NSS Cautions Kerala Government'. *The Hindu*. January 22. p. 8. Also 'A Timely Warning' (1999). *The Hindu*. December 16. p. 10.
146. Ibid.
147. T.V. Rajeshwar (1998). 'The Curse of the Caste System'. *The Hindustan Times*. November 22, p. 13.
148. Gail Omvedt (2000). 'The Purpose of Reservation–I'. *The Hindu*. March 24.
149. Susmita Dasgupta (2001). *The* Politics of Mobilisation of Backward Classes. Paper Presented at Seminar at University of Pune. p. 17

150. Ibid. Also Bipan Chandra Aditya and Mridula Mukherjee (1999). *India After Independence.* Delhi: Viking. pp. 25–35.
151. Gail Omvedt (2000). 'The Purpose of Reservation–II. *The Hindu*. March 25.
152. It continues to block a true representation of the majority of the nation's population, a representation which the founders and leaders of the anti-caste movement had always seen as part of a full-scale political socio-economic transformation. Also see Meenakshi Jain (1996). 'Backward Castes and Social Change in Uttar Pradesh and Bihar'. In M.N. Srinivas (ed.).(1996). *Caste: Its 20th Century Avtar,* Delhi: Viking. p.135.
153. M.N. Srinivas (ed.). op. cit. no. 152. p.26.
154. For details see K.P. Prabhakaran Nair (1999). 'Manu and Mandal' *The Hindu*, 3 August. Also Girish Menon (2000). 'Creamy Layer Issue: NSS Cautions Kerala Government'. *The Hindu*. January 22, p. 8. Also 'A Timely Warning' (1999). *The Hindu*. December 16, p. 10.
155. M.N. Srinivas (ed.). op. cit. no. 152. p.26. Also see Pradeep Kumar (2001). 'Identifying real Backwards and Dalits'. *The Tribune*. October 17.
156. V.P. Singh tried to put the cart before the horse in the sense that he promised reservation in jobs but he did not announce anything regarding education'. *The Hindustan Times*. (1991) January 19. Quoted in Ambeth Rajan (1994). *My Bahujan Samaj Party.* Delhi: ABCDE Publication. pp.45–46.
157. For further details see: Kanchan Chandra (1997). 'Party Strategies in the UP Assembly Elections 1996'. *Economic and Political Weekly.* February 1, p. 214. Also Nikhil Chakravarty (1991). 'Mandal Report, Narasimha Rao and V.P. Singh'. *Mainstream*. Vol. XXIX, no. 50, October 5, p. 4. Also R.C. Dutt (1993). 'The Mandal Commission'. *Mainstream*. February 13, pp.13–14.
158. M.N. Srinivas (ed.) (1996). op. cit. no. 152. Also Pradeep Kumar (1998). 'Quest for Power: Oppositional Movements and Post-Congress Politics in Uttar Pradesh'. *Seminar–471*. November, p. 73 (Book Review).
159. As quoted in Susmita Dasgupta (2001). n. 149. Also Pradeep Kumar (1994). 'Backwards Among the Backwards'. *Mainstream*. January 8, p. 24.

160. Ghanshyam Shah (2001). 'Dalit Movements and the Search for Identity' in Ghanshyam Shah (ed.), *Dalit Identity and Politics*. Delhi: Sage. pp. 209, 236, 238.
161. T.K. Oommen (1990). *Protest and Change: Studies in Social Movements*. New Delhi: Sage. p. 264.
162. Gail Omvedt (2001). 'Ambedkar and After: The Dalit Movement in India' in Ghanshyam Shah (ed.) (2001). *Dalit Identity and Politics*. New Delhi: Sage. p. 158.
163. Ghanshyam Shah (2001). op. cit. no. 91.
164. Ibid.
165. Waman Nimbalkar (1973). *Gaokushabaheril Kavita*. Translated by G. Smith and E. Zelliot. Aurangabad: Asmitadarsh Prakashan. Also Oliver Mendelson (2000). op. cit. no. 72. p. 134.
166. T.K. Oommen (1990). *Protest and Change: Studies in Social Movements*. New Delhi: Sage. p. 263.
167. They felt these problems could not be tackled through the mechanism of appeasement, 'tokenism', in the form of economic concessions or political reservation. The only way out was to capture political power.
168. T.K. Oommen (1990). op. cit. no. 166. p. 264.
169. In Karnataka, Dalit students and youth organised themselves after a rioting incident provoked by the statement of a Dalit minister that upper caste dominated Kannada literature was only *bhoosa* (cattle feed); caste Hindu students attacked Dalits and Dalits not only retaliated physically and with a poster war ('throw the Brahmans into the gutter along with Gita'), but also organised themselves in a series of local organisations that finally formed a state-wide Dalit Sangarsh Samiti in 1974.
170. Gail Omvedt (2001). op. cit. no. 162. p. 153.
171. Lata Murugkar (1991). *Dalit Panther Movement in Maharashtra: A Sociological Appraisal*. Bombay: Popular Prakashan. p. 236. Also Ghanshyam Shah (2001).op. cit. no. 164. p. 209.
172. For details see Sudha Pai (1998). 'The BSP in Uttar Pradesh'. *Seminar* 471. November. p. 38. Also Mohan Sahay (1997). 'Dalit Politics: the Relevance of Ambedkar'. *The Statesman*. August 19. Also Gopal Guru (2001). op. cit. no. 74. p. 175.

173. Out of desperation they collectively voiced the view that they had no motherland; they would give up their citizenship and shed their blood to achieve a homeland – Dalitstan. It was based on the argument that higher caste Hindus, as a majority, would persist in committing atrocities on Dalits. The demand was distinct from 'Khalistan', i.e. one for a separate Sikh nation. It was a demand for a separate village settlements of Dalits where there would not be any distinction between superior and inferior people no discrimination, no bossing, no harassment and no exploitation.
174. They further alleged that persons insisting on the use of word Dalits were encouraging casteism and classism through a literary movement.
175. In their view 'Dalitness' had become a source of confrontation of one's total being. For details see: Shaibal Gupta (1998). 'From Untouchable to Dalit'. *Bibilio: A Review of Books*. Vol. III, no. 11 & 12, November – December, p. 5. Also Jim Masselos (1983). 'Jobs and Jobbery: The Sweeper in Bombay under the Raj'. *The Indian Economic and Social History Review.* 19 (2). pp.101–35. Also Jyashree Gokhale (1993). op. cit. no. 116. pp. 65–66.
176. Oliver Mendelson (2000). op. cit. no. 72. p. 209.
177. Selig Harrison (1960). *India: The Most Dangerous Decades*. Madras: Oxford. p.191.
178. From 1952 until 1989, with the exception of the post-Emergency election of 1977, untouchables tended to function in both national and state elections as a 'vote bank' for the Congress.
179. The major examples of long-term non-Congress dominance are West Bengal, Kerala, Tamil Nadu and Andhra Pradesh.
180. Oliver Mendelson. op. cit. no. 72. p. 237.
181. The term 'Dalit Consciousness', as used here, refers to awareness of low caste identity leading to a movement in some cases. Sudha Pai (2002). *Dalit Assertion and Unfinished Democratic Revolution: The Bahujan Samaj Party in Uttar Pradesh*. New Delhi: Sage. p. 25.
182. For details see Vasant Moon (ed.) (1987). *Dr. Bhimrao Ambedkar: Writing and Speeches*. Bombay: Education Department. Govt. of Maharashtra, Vol. 3. pp. 25–30. Also Kancha Ilaiah (2001). 'Dalitism versus Brahminism: The

Epistemological Conflict in History'. In Ghanshyam Shah (ed.). *Dalit Identity and Politics*. New Delhi: Sage. pp. 121–125.

183. See Eleanor Zelliot (1998). 'The Roots of Dalit Concsciousness'. *Seminar* 471. November, p. 29.
184. See T.K. Oommen (1999). 'Dalits and Production of Knowledge–II'. *The Hindu*. September 15.
185. Ā la Gail Omvedt, Eleanor Zelliot, etc.
186. See Gopal Guru (2001). op. cit. no. 74. p. 166.
187. This particular verse reflects an epistemological point which firmly legislates that the consciousness of suffering can occur only to those who actually suffer form victimhood.
188. The impact of Tukaram on the Dalits of this region is evident form the following 'abhanga' that they seem to have used in their cultural activity.
189. This particular abhanga suggests the tradition of tolerance among Dalits who, in this phase are deriving their critical inputs from the emancipatory Nirankari traditions that fought against Brahmanical domination.
190. In Tamil and Marathi respectively.
191. Swami Achhutanand's (U.P.) and Gandhi's respectively.
192. Sheoraj Bechain (2000). 'Why not let us speak?' *The Pioneer.* January 30. Millennium p. 9.
193. Ibid.
194. See Oliver Mendelson (2000). op. cit. no. 72. p. 215.
195. He published the first paper Vital Vidhvanshan in 1888.
196. He published Somvanshiya Mitra in 1908 at Mumbai.
197. His paper called 'Chokhamela' in 1931.
198. His papers *Mooknayak* and *Bahishkrit Bharat* (Mumbai 1920, 1927).
199. P.G. Jogdanand has listed three important routes to upward social mobility among the Mahars of Maharashtra – one is by contesting and winning in the institutions of local self-governance, participation in the folk theatre like tamasha and jalsa and the third is by seeking employment in the Army. Susmita Dasgupta (2001). op. cit. no. 149. p. 11.
200. After 1970, the Dalit cultural movement was taken over by the state, in the sense that now the Khalapathak normally involved themes of family planning and prohibition which

formed part of package of various welfare schemes introduced by the state. The spread of cinema of video-culture is another important reason for the decline of Dalit cultural movement in the region. Gopal Guru (2001). op. cit. no. 74. pp. 175–179

201. Ibid., p. 181.
202. Ibid., p. 182.
203. In this 'ori' Dalit women, in their cultural polemic with high-caste women attempt to interface the cultural image of Ambedkar by imagining the golden borders on the three-piece suit of Ambedkar. They also suggest that these golden borders are much more precious than the rose of Nehru's suit.
204. The literary meaning of this 'ori' is that Ambedkar did not die a natural death but a Brahman women poisoned him through buttermilk. See Dinbandhu Bhegaonkar. (1992). *Buddha-Palana*. Bhimnagar: Akola Tathagat Publication. pp. 45–50.
205. However, the Dalit women from Marathwada who composed the 'ori' have different perception of Ambedkar's marriage with a Brahman woman and this is made clear from this 'ori'. Here the Dalit women consider the Ambedkar's marriage with a Brahman woman a matter of scoring a symbolic victory over the orthodox and obsurantist Brahmanism.
206. Gopal Guru (2001). op. cit. no. 74. p. 186.
207. Gail Omvedt (2001). *Dalit Identity and Politics*. New Delhi: Sage. p. 144.
208. From a Marathi song of the 1970s – anti-caste movement.
209. From a poem by Namdev Dhasal translated by Jayant Karve and Eleanor Zelliot in Mulkraj Anand and Eleanor Zelliot (eds.) (1992). *An Anthology of Dalit Literature*. Delhi: Gyan.
210. It has provided alternative ways of living, at some points limited and at some points radical and all-encompassing, ranging from changes in behaviour such as giving up beef eating to religious conversion.
211. As he puts it in his famous address to the Mahar railway workers at Mahad: There are in my view two enemies which the workers of the country have to deal with. The two enemies are Brahmanism and capitalism (reported in *The Times of India* 1938. February 14). The climax of this

approach, in may ways, came with the writing of 'States and Minorities', proposed to be a draft of certain sections of a constitution, wherein Ambedkar called for nationalisation of land and basic industries, explicitly calling them 'state socialism'.

212. B.R. Ambedkar (1987). 'The Buddha and his Dhamma' in V. Moon (ed.). *Dr. B.R. Ambedkar: Writings and Speeches*. Bombay: Education Department, Government of Maharashtra. Vol. II, p. 182. Also Gail Omvedt (1996). 'Ambedkar and Economics'. *Fourth World*. 3 (1).
213. Ghanshyam Shah (2001). op. cit. no. 91. p. 206.
214. Translated by Gauri Deshpande (1982) in Dilip Hero. *The Untouchables of India*. London. The Minority Rights Group. pp. 44–54.
215. Ghanshyam Shah (2001). op. cit. no. 91.
216. The word meaning 'Search for Identity'.
217. op. cit. 142, n. 263–264.
218. With this, the term 'Dalit' came into vogue. Open confrontation between Dalit Panthers and upper-caste Hindus took place several times in the 1970s. Also T.K. Oommen (1990). op. cit. no. 142. p. 263. Also Lata Murugkar (1991). op. cit. no. 171. p. 48.
219. Gopal Guru (2001). op. cit. no. 74. p. 186.
220. Gokhale-Turner (1993). op. cit. no. 116. pp. 293–335.
221. Sheoraj Bechain (2000). 'Why not let us speak?' *The Pioneer.* January 30, *Millenium*. p. 9.
222. Oliver Mendelson (2000). op. cit. no. 72. pp. 214–17. Aso Namdev Dhasal (1975). *Golpitha*. Translated by D.B. Karnik. Pune: Nilkanth Prakashan.
223. Sheoraj Bechain (2000). op. cit. no. 192. p. 9.
224. Sudha Pai (1999). *State Politics: New Dimensions*. Delhi: Shipra, pp. 173–74.
225. In the former under the leadership of the Congress and particularly Gandhi, in most of North India, social and political issues were separated and very early a model of 'harijan uplift' was established making it easier for the Congress to subsume the Dalit Movement in the immediate post-independence period. In the latter, the Dalits under Ambedkar emerged as an independent group distinct from

the non-Brahmans though they remained subordinate to the latter, which led Ambedkar to take the route of conversion to Buddhism. In contrast, in Tamil Nadu, the Dalits, while conscious of their difference, preferred to support and be a part of non-Brahmanism, attracted by the identity of 'dravidianism'.

226. Sudha Pai (1999). op. cit. no. 224. p. 174.
227. Ibid.
228. Omvedt, Gail (1992). *Dalit Visions: The Anti-Caste Movement and the Constructions of an Indian Identity.* Delhi: Orient Longman. p. 87.
229. Sudha Pai (2001). 'From Harijan to Dalit Identity Formation, Political Consciousness and Electoral Mobilization of the Scheduled Castes in Uttar Pradesh' in Ghanshyam Shah (ed.), op. cit. no. 91. p. 260.
230. For details see Francine Frankel (1977). 'Problems of Correlating Electoral and Economic Variables: An Analysis of Voting Behaviour and Agrarian Modernisation in U.P.' in M. Weiner and J.D. Fields (eds.). *Electoral Politics in the Indian States. Vol. 3. Impact of Modernisation*. Delhi: Manohar. pp. 79–84,
231. For details see next chapter. This was due to the decay and collapse of the Congress system. Brewer Stone (1988). 'Institutional Decay and the Traditionalisation of the Congress Party in U.P.'. *Asian Survey.* 28 (10). pp. 1019–20.
232. Voicing the woes of Depressed class people through their writings.
233. Sheoraj Bechain (2000). op. cit. no. 192. p. 9.
234. Ibid.
235. Surajbhan (1999). 'Daliton Ko Apne Adhikaron Ke Liye Ladna Hoga'. *Dalit Darpan*. Dehradun: Bhartiya Dalit Academy. p. 9.
236. K.K. Antiwal (1999). 'He Bheem Tumhara Abhinandan'. *Dalit Darpan*. Dehradun: Bharatiya Dalit Academy. p. 19.
237. Jai Singh Premi (1999). 'Ansu'. *Dalit Darpan*, Dehradun: Bharatiya Dalit Academy. p. 20.
238. Roop N. Sonkar (1999). 'Jab Sab Ka Malik Ek Hai'. *Dalit Darpan*. Dehradun: Bharatiya Dalit Academy, p. 23.
239. Ram Sharan Varma (1999). 'Takdir Na Badli Daliton Ki'. *Dalit Darpan*. Dehradun: Bharatiya Dalit Academy, p. 30.

240. Guru Prasad (1999). 'Jhansi Veerangana Laxmi Bai Nahi Who Jhalkari Thi'. *Dalit Darpan*. Dehradun: Bharatiya Dalit Academy. p. 24.
241. This aspect, efforts have been or are being made to activate the Dalit Consciousness; deconstruct dominant Brahmanical myths and history, explore history, caste history and glorify myths about Dalit castes as also explore the unwritten history of Dalit leaders, saints and social reformers.
242. It hopes to lead dalit culture from the realm of empiricism to that of theory, particularly a distinctive theory of knowledge.
243. This difference is evident at the levels of both form and content. Historics of the Shudras by Marxist historians are attempts to locate that group within the class framework. On the other hand, the history of Dalits and Bahujans interpret 'caste-biased' views.
244. 'Punjab's Dalits: A Divided House' (2014). *The Times of India*. November 13.
245. Sheoraj Bechain (2000). Why not let us speak?'. *The Pioneer*, January 30. Millennium. p 9. Also Dinbandhu Bhegaonkar (1992). *Buddha-Palana*. Bhimnagar: Aloka Tathagat Publication. pp. 45–50. Also B.R. Ambedkar (1987). 'The Buddha and his Dharma' in V. Moon (ed.). *Dr. B.R. Ambedkar Writings and Speeches*. Bombay: Education Department, Government of Maharashtra. Vol. II. p. 182. Also Gail Omvedt (1996). 'Ambedkar and Economics'. *Fourth World*. 3 (1).

2

Neo-Caste Realist Theory

Truth has many aspects
Infinite truth has infinite expressions

—Srimad Bhagavatam 11.15

In his radical pedagogical analysis of the 'suffering of Harijans', Brij Mohan propounded a secular aesthetico-analytic framework of a neo-casteless society.[1] Casteless society, he argued, has been built upon an egalitarian social structure with demystified vedic culture and its decadent values and practices.

Neo-caste reality theory has evolved from a self-critical phalanx of Indian scholars. A brief mention of the Dalit movement from the pre-Buddhist to the pre-Bahujan Samaj Party (BSP) phase reveals, first, how the movement gradually turned from a socio-cultural to a political one.[2] Second, in various books and also in the previous chapter, many synonyms have been used for the word 'Dalit'. Many English and Hindi words, which have been used interchangeably, need a thorough analysis to find out if there is any politics attached to its naming (and, can we build a new thought vis-à-vis their occupations?). Third, we know how the Dalit Movement evolved over the years. So, it would be pertinent to analyse whether it is more of an evolution rather than revolution (as many scholars have termed it as the latter). Fourth, much has been said about the various types of oppression the Dalits faced in the past, but the important question is, from exactly which date does this originate? Dalits do not have their own calendar. Fifth, up until now, in all literature found on Dalits, one finds the meaning confined primarily to caste oppression. By giving a broader meaning to it, can we understand the term at a trans-caste level?[3] For example, a trans-caste level would include the notion that Dalit can be understood in a new way. It is a universal concept, which includes individual, class, gender, modern slaves, nation and nature (the environment). In this way Dalit has no boundaries. It is an international concept as explained in the next chapter. Sixth, can we relate it to the political philosophy of the past and build a new philosophy that is a Dalit-political philosophy? Can we give a Dalit-dent to political philosophies whether value-laden or value-free and find a new twist and meaning in philosophy? If so, how? Finally, can we build a new political theory of dalitness, in its broader meaning and concept, and derive any important conclusions?

I have deal with the aforementioned questions, one by one, in a modest manner in this and the next chapter.

In between the pre-independence and the post-independence periods in India, under-privileged people have been called by various names, depending on the political treatment they received during different phases of history. Here we will provide a brief summary of some of the nomenclature before a more extensive discussion of the key terms.

'Achhut' (untouchable), which is one of their original names, came as a legacy of past social prejudices. Later on, the British Government called them Scheduled Castes both in the 1935 Government of India Act and in the preceding official literature. Mahatma Gandhi called them Harijans (God's children), vesting them with a semblance of divinity. However, they did not accept this super-imposed dignity. Instead they called themselves 'Dalit', 'the downtrodden', or the lowest category of the Hindus.[4] Besides untouchables, Harijans, and Dalits, other nomenclature such as depressed classes, servile classes, weaker sections, panchamas, ati-shudras, avarnas and antayajas have been employed.[5]

While the two leading terms are 'Harijan' and 'Dalit', as early as 1917, the prefix 'Adi' or 'original' was employed by untouchable leaders – who were seeking to assert their status as a people who were subordinated by the later Aryan immigrants to India.[6] The Aryans had started calling them (untouchables) *anarya* or *dasyu*. Dasyu means slave, and the Aryans started exploiting and dominating them (according to the Vedic literature). When the varna system came into existence, the dasyus became shudras or kshudra, which means the inferior caste. Hence it became the last category in the caste system (in the later Vedic period).

The negative connotations associated with the marginalized of society are evident in other nomenclature as well. For example, the word 'pariah', which derives from the Tamil name for this social group (i.e. Paraiyan), has moved into the English language as a synonym for the socially ostracized and the morally depraved.[7]

The terms used by Jyotiba Phule were 'Shudra' and 'ati-shudra'. Later, the non-Brahman movement in Maharashtra described itself as a movement of the Bahujan Samaj versus Shetji-Bhatjis.[8] The word 'Shudra' has its root in the word 'sucha', meaning sorrow.[9]

The term 'Achhut' derives from a Hindi word meaning forbidden to touch. In more modern times, Achhut has been used with a broader meaning by Shankaranad Shastri, who is a contemporary Dalit activist and writer. His works can be taken as representative of the feelings of the educated depressed classes of his time.[10] He held that the term 'Achhut' was used by the depressed classes in their struggle to imply 'pure' or 'untouched', thus giving it a new radical meaning.[11]

The term *Harijan* was first used by Narsinh Mehta, who was a 17th-century poet, saint and reformer of Gujarat, which was later popularized by Gandhi in the 20th century.[12] Mahatma Gandhi adopted the term 'Harijan' in 1933 as the winning entry in a national competition for a suitable name to replace the terms noted in the second category below.[13] Gandhi had expressed the hope with the aim of 'probably Antayaja brethren would lovingly accept that name and try to cultivate the virtues which it connotes ... may the antayaja become Harijans in name and nature'.[14] Harijan was generally accepted both by the upper and the lower castes, but in recent years it has been replaced by the term Dalit. The least attractive term is 'ex-untouchable'.[15]

The term 'Scheduled Castes' was used as a standard expression in the Indian Constitution. This term was first coined by the Simon Commission and embodied in the Government of India Act – in 1935.[16] Until that time, they were known as untouchables, depressed classes or exterior castes. The term 'SC' was used by the British[17] in a legal and administrative sense. At present, the so-called 'Schedule' is a list of castes entitled to parliament seats, public employment and special education benefits.

The word Dalit was not familiar for the lower castes in Uttar Pradesh (UP) before the Bahujan Samaj Party (BSP) popularized the term in the last two-and-a-half decades or so,[18] so that it has replaced Harijan or simply Scheduled Castes. The term 'Dalit' is commonly used in many international academic studies, seminars and conferences.[19] In recent years, few politicians in the country have discarded the Dalit category as a socially reactionary and negative one and sought to replace it with the 'Bahujan' category,[20] but the term 'Dalit' is being currently used for and by untouchables all over the country.[21]

The word 'Dalit' is originally culled from *Dalan*. Dalit means socially and culturally oppressed groups, mainly the untouchable castes.[22] In Maharashtra, where the word was first used to connote the socio-cultural movement (Dalit Panthers), it has undergone a sea change.[23] The term referred not only to caste 'but also was a symbol of change and revolution'.[24] The publication of journals in the 1980s indicates the increasing degree of Dalit Consciousness (DC) and Dalit intellectual activity in India. Most of the articles were written by Dalits who had become conscious of their rights as they had faced so much oppression and deprivation in the past. In 1981, *Dalit Voice* – a journal of Dalit Sahitya Academy – was started.[25] It presented other minorities and Backward Classes also as Dalit.

The category 'Dalit' was first used by Ambedkar himself in his fortnightly *Bahishkrit Bharat*, in which he explained that the Dalits faced social, economic, cultural and political marginalization by the upper castes.[26] Some influential scholars have employed other terminology or 'Dalit' differently. Ashish Nandy treats the category of 'Dalit' as a social construction of the middle class, which defines it in purely inscriptive terms.[27]

Harold Issac has used the category of ex-untouchables in his study.[28] Barbara Joshi and Lelah Dushkin, leading scholars on the Dalit question, use the categories of ex-untouchables and Scheduled Castes interchangeably with Dalit.[29]

Another political term that is sometimes used today is Bahujan. This name is used as a political tool in contemporary politics in north India, especially Uttar Pradesh (UP).

Regardless of the name: Dalit, Scheduled Castes, untouchables and so on, the predominate aspect that has defined their lives is the type of work they have been assigned. In fact, the menial jobs were all left to the Dalits. They cremated the dead while suffering insults, humiliation, oppression and discrimination. The Dalits have had to contend themselves with accepting their servile position. They inherited nothing but poverty, disease, misery and unemployment. Their mere shadow was considered pollution by the upper-caste Hindus. According to Vaishistha Dharamasutra, a Shudra was like a burial ground; hence Veda should never be recited in his presence.[30] Munshi Premchand's 'Sadagati' is another example of the state of lower castes.

There are two pertinent points about the usage of the term Dalit and its synonyms. First, they were given a variety of names as per their place in the social order vis-à-vis their occupation. Second, the nomenclature itself was a political tool of pre- and post-colonial leaders.

I choose to analyse both these points – in order to raise a question. Can the rise of a lower caste party (over the years) in the political stream be considered or understood as a 'revolution' as we have studied in the socio-political history of the Dalit movement? Is there any evidence that the rise of a lower caste party reflects any kind of transformation in Indian society? For example, the advent of the BSP in UP has brought some positive political transformation in society, but problems of social and economic inegalitarianism still prevail. In the following, I discuss the most troublesome problem of the Dalit, that is 'scavenging', through a case study to prove that intra-caste changes vis-à-vis occupations are on the rise and that major problems persist at the intra-caste level.

Let me first take up the case of manual scavenging. This term describes the job of Dalits that consists of removing human excrement from dry toilets and sewers using basic tools such as thin boards, buckets and baskets carried on their heads. This was banned in 1993 but the political will to enforce the ban has been lacking. In 2007, a committee of experts of the International Labour Organization (ILO) urged the Indian Government to 'take decisive action to eradicate manual scavenging and to report on nation and state-wise action to put an end to this practice and on the progress made in the identification, liberation and rehabilitation of scavengers' (DalitMarch.org/manual-scavenging.html), but this rotten practice continues to the present day. It is a basic obstacle for achieving human rights.

A Supreme Court ruling in May 2009 brought an end to this abhorrent practice a little bit closer for 1.3 million Dalits, but not soon enough. In fact, the mindset of upper-caste Indians needs to be changed to stop this degrading job. Rural Development Minister, Jairam Ramesh, had proposed projects worth $130 million to rid India of the scourge of open defecation and to clean up a rail system, which he described as the world's 'largest open toilet'. Approximately 4,00,000–5,00,000 children, under five, die each year from diarrhoea in India 'largely caused by unhygienic practices, including improper disposal of human excreta'.[31]

Manual scavenging continues to be a national shame.[32] Two Dalits died of asphyxiation while cleaning a sewage tank in a private hotel in Tamil Nadu. The debasing occupation, forced chiefly on Dalits through their descent, prompted the Supreme Court, recently, to make stinging comments against the Union Government for 'not enacting a law that will ban manual scavenging'. According to a census data, there are 7,50,000 families involved in manual scavenging in the country.[33]

The problem of open defecation and dealing with human excrement is a crucial health concern for the government. As many as 67 per cent of households in rural India defecate in the open and several states 'fudge' data on the building of toilets. Drinking Water and Sanitation Minister, Jairam Ramesh said that during Question Hour if states were to be believed, 60 per cent of households in rural India have been provided toilets, but according to the 2011 census only 33 per cent have the facility.[34] It is puzzling to realize that it has taken 66 years for our rulers to pass a bill to ban this practice in September 2013.[35]

The law passed by the Indian Parliament banned the practice of manual scavenging. According to the Prohibition of Employment as Manual Scavengers and the Rehabilitation Act, every local authority, housing board and railway authority has to survey latrines within their respective jurisdictions in order to identify manual scavengers. The law suggests owners should be held responsible for the conversion of dry latrines into sanitary ones with a flush system. Current workers are supposed to be reassigned and provided with housing assistance and training to develop alternative employment opportunities. Social Justice Minister Kumari Selja said, 'This dehumanizing practice is inconsistent with the right to live with dignity'. One may well wonder why this problem was not taken seriously all these years by various political parties?

The BJP's Prime Ministerial candidate, Narendra Modi, had a mantra 'toilets first, temples later' that had irked the VHP Chief, Parveen Togadia, the Bajrang Dal activists, and others also; but, this statement shows Modi's foresight to solve the problem (scavenging) from the root.

Moreover, proper toilets and plumbing could also protect rural women to some extent. In a few rape cases, it was found that the victims were grabbed when they went out of the house, which had no toilet. It is pertinent to mention the UN Secretary General Ban Ki-moon's statement regarding the Badaun (Uttar Pradesh) victims' case: 'In the last two weeks we have seen despicable attacks against women around the world. I was appalled by rape and murder of two teenagers in India who ventured out as they had no access to toilet ... .' (*The Times of India*, 5 June 2014). It should be noted that the Central Bureau of Investigation (CBI) filed a closure report in the Badaun Case, where they ruled out murder and rape, and concluded that it was a case of suicide. This finding has been questioned (*The Times of India*, 12 December 2014).

In the preceding chapter, we discussed the Dalit Movement (DM) through various phases. The case of manual scavenging proves that the problem of oppression of the Dalits is still alive. I will discuss the genesis and political performance of the

Bahujan Samaj Party (BSP) later, but the fact remains that political power has surely not been a key to ban all social evils, as social and economic inegalitarianism persists.

Although inequality continues for the Dalits, but due to the political accomplishments of the BSP, there has been some suggestion that a revolution has taken place in India. For example, in the respective books of the three authors Gail Omvedt's,[36] *Dalits and the Democratic Revolution*, Sudha Pai's[37] *Dalit Assertion and the Unfinished Democratic Revolution*, and Christophe Jaffrelot's[38] *India's Silent Revolution: The Rise of Lower Castes in India*, there is a common word in the title of each book that the Dalit achievement of political power means that there has been a revolution. One may rightfully ask, however, whether this better described as a revolution or evolution? To my understanding, it is the latter. Revolution is normally understood to mean there has been a fundamental change in power or organizational structures that takes place in a relatively short period of time. They seek not only a new political system but transform an entire society. In contrast, the Dalit Movement took birth and has gained momentum, albeit slowly. Many other movements petered out due to various reasons, the Dalit political movement advanced in various phases. Dalits gained political power only after a long period of fighting for their rights, which cannot, in my view, be termed a revolution.

Even if one considers it (democratic revolution) to be a slow revolution, the fact is it has not brought any sweeping transformation to Indian society either. No political regime was overthrown by any popular movement. In Bjorn Thomassen's view, the Dalit rise to political power can better be termed as 'liminal movement'. This would not only imply a focus on political behaviour 'from below', but also recognize moments where 'high and low' are relativized, and where the micro and macro levels fuse together in critical conjunctions.[39]

The study and analysis of the DM both in the colonial and in post-colonial periods (as discussed in Chapter 1) reveals the process of change has been gradual. In between the movement even petered out, and again evolved. The latest political rise of Dalits in India with the advent of the BSP in the state of UP in 1985 has been due to gradual evolution since it took birth as a non-political body in 1978 to serve the interests of Dalits and minority communities (see discussion in Chapter 4). They have gained power and support gradually, especially in Uttar Pradesh. However, that evolution has failed to transform the entire society; here, I mean, especially, the mindset of the upper castes.

Before concluding this chapter, I would like to raise an important question for readers to ponder. While the traditional functions of all four castes are well known, what has been the effect of globalization, vis-à-vis Indian citizens, within and outside India? Have they not transcended the boundaries of caste functions? Is there a neo-caste post-structured way of adopting new roles?

It is true that trans-caste occupations are on the rise. One of the reasons is the rising emphasis on materialism and growing demands of each member within a family for more material goods. For instance, there are cases where an upper-caste Indian is now employed in toilet cleaning and sweeping in India and abroad because of the need to earn some kind of income. In India, we find such cases mostly in hotels or shopping malls. There are also examples of an upper-caste employee in a hospital whose daily job includes cleaning patients' excreta. On the other hand, we find low-caste Indians holding top positions in office service or business in India.

One new emerging trend, beyond caste lines, is that today occupation has also become hereditary. We find that few individuals (irrespective of any caste factor) do not follow the occupation of caste stratifications (as laid by Manu, the law giver), but are more interested in following the occupation of their parents for better and sudden economic gains, like an actor's son or daughter embarking on a acting career because they receive favours based on nepotism, or a politician's son or daughter following in the same occupation. So it is not the new generation of B, K, V, and S being B, K, V, S, but a particular/same occupation being followed by the next generation has a new pattern. So, as compared to the traditional view, given in Table II, Table I highlights differences in three respects. First, while in Table II, occupation was hereditary apropos caste lines, in Table I it is hereditary on trans-caste lines. Second, another factor of change is in the traditional view of Table I, the occupational movement is only vertical, while in Table II it is both vertical as well as horizontal. Third, in Table

II, the occupational movement was male oriented while in Table I, it includes both genders.

Table I

Newly Emerged Occupational Pattern (Trans-caste and beyond BKVS including both genders and horizontal and vertical mobility)

1.	Politician (example of vertical mobility of occupation)	Daughter/Son politician
2.	Male actor	Daughter actor (example of occupational mobility which is not male oriented as in Table II – Traditional view.)
3.	Politician (husband) example of horizontal mobility of occupation	Politician (wife)

Even in the matrimonial columns in the newspapers for people to search for a possible groom or bride there are two types of advertisements: one for caste and another for occupation. It is also true of Internet matrimonial sites where one has to give his/her preferences regarding caste and occupation. The first depicts the search for a partner on the basis of a common caste and the second one is on the basis of occupation. It seems that the latter is given more and more preference. One of the reasons for this is the simple economic requirements in a world of increasing consumerism.

Another point that can be raised is how we can understand the term 'Dalit' or the social structure vis-à-vis an individual's daily chores? Does it have any effect on caste hierarchy? After all, it is individuals that form society. A popular understanding of caste hierarchy is concerned with the social functions and roles performed by individuals born in a particular caste family. However, a person belonging to any caste, at the individual level also, performs functions for himself/herself. So, it is useful to consider an individual's daily chores and then proceed to think about his or her duties for society. An interesting question that may provoke further thought is, 'Can these functions as an individual and for society make any dent in caste hierarchy?' If yes, what effect will it have on the individual and societal level?

Consider, for example, the kind of duties many people perform every day, regardless of caste. The mother of a (baby) whose daily routine includes cleaning of excreta, or children cleaning excreta of their bedridden parents/siblings. Such tasks are considered a traditional job of a Shudra/Dalit. This task is even worse than a shudra's as the former has to even clean the body parts of a child/patient. By and large, this is performed happily by family members as a moral duty. Or what about going to a temple or praying (which is a function of a Brahman)? Another example would be earning bread for his/her family (which is function of a Vaishya) – or looking after one's own and the family's security (which is the function of a Kshatriya). From this perspective, all traditional castes and functions as given by Manu can be understood first at the individual level and then be related to society. Moreover, in my view, a consideration of an individual's chores and functions versus caste functions can be the foundation for re-examining caste and offering a neo-caste realist approach (see Table III). Narrowing down the understanding of caste from the division of society to the divisions of work by any caste individual in their daily and familial tasks can provide the impetus to change everyone's mindset vis-à-vis lower castes and bring about equality in society (in practice).

It can be understood in the following way as shown in Tables II and III.

Table II

Neo-caste Realist Theory

1. Traditional View	*2. Modern View*
Caste Functions	Any Caste (*Daily functions) Individual
Brahman – to pray	(a) Toilet cleaning For himself or for others
Kshatriya – to fight	(b) Praying
Vaishya – to produce	(c) Going to earn
Shudra – menial works	(d) Taking care of himself/family's security

* Daily functions apropos both traditional and modern view correspond to four castes.

Table III

New Liberal Caste Approach

Caste	*Steps/Functions*
1. Shudra	Toilet cleaning for himself or others
2. Brahman	Praying
3. Vaishya	Going to earn
4. Kshatriya	Taking care of his/family security

Steps/Functions in the above-mentioned Table IIII may interchange as per the individual's choice

This neo-realistic individual functions approach is based on the fact that the lowest caste functions are performed by almost everyone regardless of caste. Further can we build a neo-caste liberal meaning of Dalit and attempt to build a theory by applying this liberal meaning to the past and the contemporary philosophies of political scholars? The next chapter attempts to do so.

Notes

1. B. Mohan (1972). *India's Social Problems: Analyzing Basic Issues*. Allahabad: India International Publications.
2. Priti Nath (2001). 'Politics of Radical Transformation'. Paper presented in a seminar on Social Oppression and the Emancipatory Project. 27–28 February. Panjab University, Chandigarh.
3. It can be something akin to narrow and broader meanings of non-violence that Mahatma Gandhi gave. The literal meaning of the term nonviolence connotes no indulgence in physical violence. It was Gandhi who widened the meaning and included (non-violence) in thought, word and deed too.
4. Arvind Das (2000). 'Silence of the Wolves'. *The Pioneer Magazine*. 30 January. p. 3.
5. Rebati Ballav Tripathi (1994). *Dalits: A Sub-human Society*. Delhi: Ashish. p. 2.
6. Oliver Mendelson and Marika Vicziany (2000). *The Untouchables*. Delhi: Cambridge University Press. p. 3.

7. Michael Moffatt (1979). *An Untouchable Community in South Asia*. Princeton, NJ: Princeton University Press. p. 6.
8. Gail Omvedt (2001). 'Ambedkar and After: The Dalit Movement in India', in Ghanshyam Shah (ed.). *Dalit Identity and Politics*. New Delhi: Sage. p. 158.
9. K.P. Prabhakaran Nair (1999). 'Manu and Mandal'. *The Hindu*. 3 August.
10. Sudha Pai (2002). *Dalit Assertion and Unfinished Democratic Revolution: The Bahujan Samaj Party in Uttar Pradesh*. New Delhi: Sage. p. 163.
11. Ibid.
12. For details see Ghanshyam Shah. no. 8. p. 21.
13. Oliver Mendelson (2000). op. cit. no. 6. p. 3.
14. Ghanshyam Shah (ed.). *Dalit Identity and Politics*. New Delhi. Sage. p. 21. Also see M.K. Gandhi (1971). *Collective Works of Mahatma Gandhi*. Delhi: Publication Division. Vol. 47. pp. 244–245.
15. Oliver Mendelson and Marika Vicziany (2000). *The Untouchables*. Delhi: Cambridge University Press. p. 255.
16. Rebati Ballav Tripathi (1994). *Dalits: A Sub-human Society*. Delhi: Ashish. p. 37.
17. Lloyd I. Susane Rudolph and Hober Rudolph (1969). *The Modernity of Tradition*. Delhi: Orient Longman. p. 133.
18. Pradeep Kumar (1999). 'BSP Breaking Ground Realities in Uttar Pradesh'. *Mainstream*. 1 May. p. 18.
19. Gopal Guru (2001). 'The Language of Dalit-Bahujan Political Discourse', in Ghanshyam Shah (ed.). *Dalit Identity and Politics*. New Delhi: Sage. p. 107.
20. Baburao Bagul (ed.) (1981). *Dalit Sahitya Ajche Kranti Vidnayan* (Marathi). Nagpur: Buddhist Publishing House. pp. 221–223.
21. Nandu Ram (1995). *Beyond Ambedkar*. Delhi: Har Anand. p. 18.
22. Desai (1985). *Caste, Caste Conflict and Reservation*. Delhi: Eastern. p. 152.
23. Lata Murugkar (1988). 'Dalit Literacy Movement in Maharashtra and Dalit Movement'. Paper presented in a seminar on 'Dalit Literature'. Centre for Social Studies. Surat.
24. Opined by Marathi Dalit activist – Gangadhar Pantawane.

25. Ganshyam Shah's article (2001). 'Dalit Movement and the Search for Identity', in Ghanshyam Shah (ed.). *Dalit Identity and Politics*. New Delhi: Sage. p. 210.
26. Dr Babasaheb Amdebkar (1990). *Yancha Bahishkrit Bharat aur Muknayak*. Education Department. Bombay: Government of Maharashtra. pp. 194–198.
27. Ashish Nandy (1988). Speech at United Theological College. Bangalore. 29 July.
28. Harold Issac (1965). *Ex-Untouchables*. Bombay: Asia Publication.
29. Barbara R. Joshi (1982). *Democracy in Search of Equality*. Delhi. National. pp. 15–20.
30. Vaishistha Dharamasutra. 18. pp. 11–15.
31. Jai Ram Ramesh.
32. R. Ilangovan. 'Death in Gutter'. *Frontline*. 31 May 2013. p. 1.
33. 'Manual Scavenging Figures Shocking, Says Jairam'. *The Hindu*. 10 June 2012. Also see Tripti Nath (2011). 'India's Shunned Latrine Cleaners Toil Despite Ban'. We.News. 6 February.
34. 'States Fudging Data, Taking Money but Not Building Toilets: Jairam Ramesh'. *PTI*. 14 August 2012. 14.54 IST.
35. See *The Hindustan Times*. 8 September 2013. p. 1.
36. Gail Omvedt (1994). *Dalits and the Democratic Revolution*. Delhi. Sage.
37. Sudha Pai (2002). Dalit Assertion and Unfinished Democratic Revolution: The Bahujan Samaj Party in Uttar Pradesh. New Delhi: Sage. p. 163.
38. Christophe Jafferlot (2002). *India's Silent Revolution: The Rise of Lower Castes in North India*. Delhi: Permanent Black.
39. Thomassen, Bjorn (2012). 'Toward an Anthropology of Political Revolutions'. *Comparative Studies in Society and History*. 54 (3). pp. 679–706.

3

Dalit Philosophy

A Trans-Caste Concept

> We are addicted to our thoughts.
> We cannot change anything if we cannot change our thinking.
>
> —Santosh Kalwar

Any theory or philosophy on Dalit epistemology, essentially, needs a holistic approach. Before constructing a new meaning, let me stick to its genesis, that is, Dalit meaning *Dalan* 'ground down to pieces' – a social fact in the traditional caste system. Can we relate this meaning to philosophical intertextuality?[1] The argument is that I wish to explain Dalit politics through the lens of intertextuality that has, normally, never been discussed in any text till date. I would like to draw a different view point of the concept through deconstruction.[2] How can the Dalit structure, built out of the structure of caste, create a new concept? How it makes sense in relation by beginning from an individual's soul, mind, heart and ending in social groups, nation and modern political theories. This will be both casual (already understood meaning) and non-casual that I would attempt to derive from a type of anti-foundationlist position.[3]

In this chapter, I would like to apply the meaning of Dalit/*Dalan* oppression to various political philosophies and see how it fits into giving a broader meaning of oppression both in value-laden and empirical sense, to draw some kind of rationale in Dalit paradigm.

Plato's *Republic* (written in 360 BC)[4] centres on a simple question – is it always better to be just than unjust? His principle of ideal justice with 'J' (capital) vice 'j' means each class in society doing its own role, without interfering with the other. And to explain this he draws an analogy of the 'just' individual and the 'just' state. Men of gold, silver and copper corresponding to ruling military and producer class, resulting from qualities of soul – reason, spirit and appetite.

To explain Dalit 'oppression' in the Platonian sense, one quality of soul here is dominating or we can say oppressing the other, which is leading to three different classes.

In yet another sense (not Plato's), every individual (universally true) is supposed to take decisions regarding his or her own actions as well as the actions of others. And for this he or she faces a tussle between the heart and the mind. In some, the heart oppresses the mind and for others it is vice versa.

Here, one can explain the kind of *Dalan*/oppression heart, mind and soul face. Whereas applying *Dalan*/oppression to Plato's theory is totally hypothetical and value-laden, the heart-mind tussle explained vis-à-vis individual's actions – is an absolute truth.

Let us now see if we can find any kind of oppression in Aristotle's theory[5] in *The Politics*. His views on family, in which he discusses the master-slave, husband-wife and parents-children relationships, clearly indicate a kind of oppression/*Dalan* by the master, the husband, the parents on the slaves, wife and the children respectively. Aristotle condones the exclusion of women from civic affairs because this practice conforms to the natural complementarity of the sexes and because it, naturally, fortifies the pluralistic structure of the society.[6] In fact, only the adult male citizens were allowed to have a political say in the state, thereby disallowing women, children, slaves and foreigners. So, one finds another example of political *Dalan*/oppression.

An analysis of social contract theories by Hobbes, Locke and Rousseau also gives a glimpse of *Dalan*/oppression, namely in Thomas Hobbes'[7] greatest work *Leviathan*, he says that the human being is, perpetually, seeking after something. 'Life itself is but motion ...' (*Leviathan*, 87). He pictures a state of nature where all are at war against all. Everyone is living in a fearful state based on the notion of might is right. Thus, one finds typical oppression, based on the strength (physical).

For John Locke,[8] the state of nature faced a problem of insecurity in the absence of legislature, executive and judiciary. So, only those who could dominate could interpret natural rights. Here the/oppression was present, but in a different form.

Rousseau, in his theory, sees no room for right, law and morality due to progress of science and arts. Private property was a source of inequality, mutual dependence and jealousy. Again, one finds oppression and suppression due to 'mine and thine' approach of those who owned property over those who did not.

In all the above theories, *Dalan* of various classes is prevalent due to various factors, thereby meaning that Dalit comprehension should transcend caste and we must have a holistic approach to it. The oppression in social contract theory of Hobbes was of higher degree (propounder of Absolute sovereignty), and the least in Rousseau[9] (advocate of popular sovereignty, whereas Locke attained the middle position [Limited sovereignty]).

In today's world of the degradation of moral values, it is sad to hear *Dalan* of one's own blood relations (family members) due to various reasons which, by and large, goes unreported.

In Marxism,[10] Marx's class theory asserts that an individual's position, within a class hierarchy, is determined by his or her role in the production process and argues that political and ideological consciousness is determined by class position. According to Karl Marx, 'The history of all hitherto existing society is the history of class struggles ... Freeman and Slave, patrician and plebian, lord and serf, guild-master and journeyman, a word oppressor and oppressed, stood in constant opposition to each other – society splitting into two classes, the Bourgeois and Proletariat' (Community Manifesto).

If we analyse this theory, we understand that it was the 'haves' who constantly oppressed the 'have nots'. The poor were oppressed and exploited. So the word Dalit should be understood in class sense also, that is, exploitation/oppression of the poor by the rich class. In the present day also, the Marxist theory of exploitation by state holds true.

So far the political philosophers we discussed were mostly those who wrote hypothetical theories or half-hypothetical theories. Coming to propounders of modern democracy[11] – it's the elite theory, which seeks to describe and explain the power relationships in contemporary society. While Vilfredo Pareto emphasized the psychological and intellectual superiority of elites (minority rule of governing elites over majority of non-governing elites was based on this), G. Mosca talks of the sociological and personal characteristics of elites who are an organized minority ruling over unorganized majority.

Analysing the oppression in both the above theories, we find that (i) there is a clear distinction of exploitation of minority ruling political class (if corrupt) over non-political majority class; (ii) there exists a psychological oppression/*Dalan* of ruling class over another who claim to be intellectually sociologically and personally superior to others; and (iii) this kind of political and psychological oppression is more in views of Pareto than of Mosca[12] as the former advocates horizontal mobilization and the latter vertical mobilization of the political elite.

Robert Michels[13] developed the Iron Law of Oligarchy, in which he asserts that all organizations were elitist. Hence, oppression of various types is present – a la political, economic, social, cultural and religious – vis-à-vis within the type of organization a person belongs to.

So, the word Dalit – which till now is, generally, understood as the lowest caste – must not be overlooked in the aforementioned ways, which give it a broader base of comprehension. Another kind of oppression/*Dalan* that cannot be ignored is based on gender, especially, in India's patriarchal society. Though the idea of 'powerful' women has retained visibility, India still is home of unspeakable crimes against women. Crimes such as rape, molestation, dowry deaths, few khap panchayat rulings, honour killings, murders, acid attacks and so on are all on the rise. Reporting of crime tends to be incomplete, so the data are prima facie suspect.[14] In fact, the 2012 'Nirbhaya' incident turned out to be an inspiration for a movement demanding respect for women.[15] This incident brought together thousands of people demanding justice and execution of a strict law for the first time in India. This implies a gender orientation of the term Dalit/*Dalan*. It reveals how, over the centuries, women have faced exploitation and are still being oppressed due to brutal crimes. From the gender point of view, it is the female oppression/*Dalan* by the male counterpart. Conversely, we cannot ignore cases of women in crime and the latest example is that of the Naxalite with women majority in its brigade, which led to the Bastar bloodbath. It was an attack on the Congress leaders and party workers. So gender-based *Dalan*/oppression can be both ways.[16]

Another example of gender oppression (not on their male counterparts but on public in general) is of female terrorists being used by most wanted terrorist[17] organizations. Apropos TV/print media news of mid-August 2013, one of the most wanted terrorists, Abdul 'Kunda', planned to use a 'breast bomb' by implanting it in a lady terrorist to blow up an aerodrome or aeroplane. This type of incident can result in high alert situation in India and abroad. This crime, if committed, shows how women in crime oppress or ground down the innocent human beings. It clearly depicts another type of *Dalan*.

Another kind of oppression could be of corrupt[18] politicians vis-à-vis the innocent citizens. Such kind of movement against corruption was spearheaded by Baba Ramdev,[19] Arvind Kejriwal, Anna Hazare[20] and now the present members of Aam Admi Party (AAP). So, it explains the oppression of non-corrupt majority by a corrupt political minority. The 2011 Anti-Corruption Movement in India included a series of demonstrations and protests across the country. It intended to establish strong legislation and enforcement against endemic political corruption before the 2012 Indian anti-corruption movement kick-started. The chief aim of the movement was to alleviate corruption of the Indian Government through the Jan Lok Pal Bill.[22] Another important aim of the movement, led by protests under Swami Ramdev, was the repatriation of black money from Swiss and foreign banks. But tear gas shells were fired by the police, and many innocent people were hurt and hospitalized. Thus, the innocent people were oppressed badly in a democratic country. Likewise Anna Hazare too asked people to wage a decisive war against corruption and to vote consciously.

So, through all these examples, a very broad meaning of the word Dalit is drawn. This kind of oppression is found in philosophies and thoughts of scholars, and it is also prevalent in various ways in India. So, mainly *Dalan*/Dalit of two kinds can be understood: intra-national and inter-national.

The first has already been discussed at length. The latter can be understood largely from various perspectives. The first perspective is India as a colony of the British. At this stage of the colonial era, one witnessed *Dalan*/oppression[21] of Indians by foreigners. The second perspective is the post-colonial era of neo-colonization.[22] The third perspective is India's image of being a 'soft' state. In all the aforementioned points I have made, oppression of the majority by a few is the primary focus to explain the idea of Dalit/*Dalan*/oppression outside the parameters of caste. Though Britain's relationship with India was of political subordination, we find three more types of exploitations[23] during the period of mercantilism, free trade and finance imperialism. Dadabhai Naoroji's drain of wealth theory explains that poverty of India was the direct consequence of continuous drain of our country's wealth in British hands. So by the time we got independence, the great problem we faced was of underdevelopment[24] and how to go in for nation-building.

Contemporary India is an example to explain neo-colonialism. How socio-economic and political control is,[25] somehow, being exercised economically, linguistically and culturally, whereby the promotion of the culture of the neo-colonist country facilitates the cultural assimilation of the colonized people (India) and thus has opened the national economy to the multinational corporations (MNCs) of the neo-colonial[26] country today.

This explains the domination: praxis. It is akin to imperial and hegemonic varieties of colonialism, practiced by Britain in the past.

It is pertinent to explain here the dependency theory between the centre and periphery[27] model in international relations, which clearly explain the levels of exploitation of the Third World countries by the First World countries – that is, centre of centre exploiting most of the peripheries of the periphery countries (to the highest degree). The centre of centre includes most of the developed countries who have a dominant say in international organizations in which counties in the periphery (both developing and the under-developed) are also members. The latter have to be succumb to the pressure of the former in various ways at international stage vis-à-vis any agenda like environment pollution, terrorism, permanent membership in UN, aid and so on.

The analysis of the above two examples leads to two conclusions:

First *Dalan* oppression of Indians in the past by the British and at present through neo-colonial phase, which encompasses Indians of all castes, class, creed, colour and sex (no discrimination is made on this basis). Two, the core countries continue to remain oppressors and periphery, the suppressed of the former. Here *Dalan*/being grounded by rich countries is an example to show how broadly the word *Dalan*/Dalit can be understood vis-à-vis oppression.

In South Asia, India is considered a fumbling 'soft state'[28] despite its size and economy. One important reason of India's[29] inability to exercise its clout is 'we keep silent and accept whatever comes our way'. With Modi's emergence as a man of practical vision, it's vehemently hoped by the commoners and the connoisseurs that India will, at last, shed the image of being a soft state by any stretch of imagination.

Here again, the example of India being suppressed/ oppressed by neighbouring countries shows that to understand the word Dalit, we must not narrow it down only to caste. It may be at a larger level of sovereign albeit oppressed nation. Apropos a news report, the first Global Slavery Index has estimated that 13.3–14.7 million people live like slaves in India[30] (out of 26.6 million total across the world). Modern slavery includes traditional slaves, those in debt bondage, forced labour or forced marriage and kids sold as victims of trafficking.

The above discussion to understand the word Dalit can be put in a utopian sense – in short – the qualities of soul oppressing each other (as per Plato's view) resulting in corresponding classes of state and tussle of heart and mind where only one rules for 'self' and 'other' regarding actions. So this idea of suppression becomes a habit of mind or heart in an individual. The state of nature by social contracturalists also depicts social oppression. For Marx, it is the class oppression.[31] Elitist theorists[32] of democracy believe in oppression of the ruled by the ruling. At the international level, we have examples of oppressed nations.

So, what have we arrived at by stating the above example? That our comprehension of the word Dalit, only in the caste sense, is a very narrow perspective. It can be understood more clearly through Table IV.

Table IV

The Trans-caste Dalit Philosophy

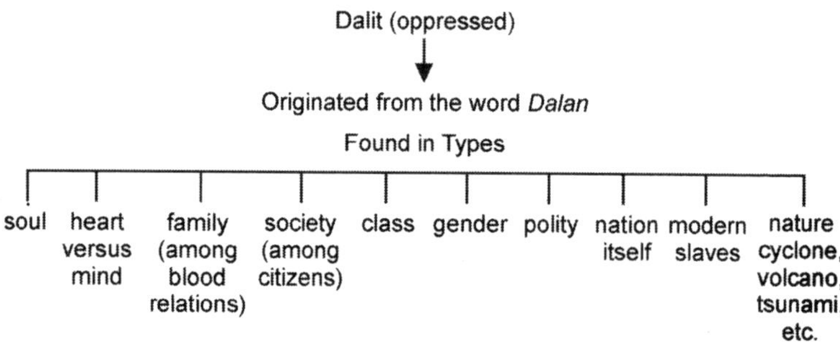

So, in the individual sense, it includes the nature of oppression by soul, heart or mind. At the societal level, it includes caste, class, gender or any kind of social organization.

Most behavioural theorists[33] have talked about new concepts such as power,[34] political system, structural-functional approach,[35] authority,[36] legitimacy,[37] political communication theory and so on. The common thread underlying all these concepts or theories is political power only. Why is it that till now – despite so much that has been written on Dalit, caste, its movements and problems – no theory or philosophy on Dalit has been made? Is it due to academic-upper-caste-oppression? Or, is it an effect of 'academic colonialism'[38] that we write only on theories or subjects that are a fad in the Western world?

When we agree that there is an iron law of oligarchy, then why cannot we accept there is an iron law of dalitness/oppression, which is found right from the individual level vis-à-vis his actions to family and all social organizations, ending at the state and at the international level too. Here one cannot ignore another type of *Dalan* by nature in the form of tsunami, earthquake, floods, eruption of volcanoes, cyclone or like the tragedy of Kedarnath,[39] in which innocent people were either swept away or hurt. It reveals that our state's disaster management is still poor. This explains a typical type of *Dalan* of all affected people (whether in their personal life they are oppressors or oppressed) by various geographical phenomena on which even today we have no control.

If we compare and analyse the degree of trans-caste Dalan in various types mentioned in Table VI, we find an interesting conclusion in Table V. It depicts the various degrees (from highest, mid-range to the lowest) of oppression that people face with reasons relating to the same.

Table V

Degree of Dalan in Trans-Caste Model

	Degree	*Type of Dalan*	*Reason*
1.	Worst	Own blood relations, Nature's (environment) fury	Difficult to cure
2.	Medium	Class, gender, society polity, nation	Not difficult to endure
3.	Least	Prevalent in every individual's soul, heart and mind	Individual himself/herself responsible for it can be cured.

Table VI clearly depicts few cases of *Dalan* within the systems in which we live and interact a la political, social, domestic, religious, media and so on. This includes both at the national and the international level. Real justice for Dalits can be brought if such cases or problems do not occur at all. This is possible if one realizes the importance of M.K. Gandhi's quote: 'There is a higher court of justice, that is the court of conscience. It supersedes all other courts'.

Such is our mindset that the moment we hear the word Dalit, we cannot think of anything else but caste. In fact, it is just an adjective used to denote the lowest caste. A heuristic understanding requires an in-depth approach, which

Table VI

Trans-Caste Dalan at a Glance (few cases)
Including Various Systems at National and International Levels

Type of System and Year	*Case*	*Plaintiff/Pertaining to*	*Pressure by*	*Result/Consequences*
		National Level		
2013[40] Religion	Of spiritual leader Asaram	Complaints by parents of inmate of Chindwara Gurukul in MP	Its own sect, media and citizens activism	Arrested by Jodhpur Police from his ashram in Indore
2013 Religion	Renowned spiritual leader[41] Narain Sai	Case of two sisters (2002–2005) in his city-based ashram and his hatching a conspiracy to bribe police to weaken the case	Media, police and citizen activism	Taken to custody after nearly two months
2012–2013 Social	Nirbhaya[42]	Horrific crime in moving bus	Gender activists, media and politicians	New law framed Accused arrested
2013 Judiciary	Justice A. K. Ganguly's[43]	By law intern at a hotel in Central Delhi	All India Democratic Women's Association (AIDWA), All India Progressive Women's Association (AIPWA), National Federation of Indian Women (NFIW)	Memorandum addressed to the PM, demanding the removal of the judge

Cont'd...

...*Cont'd*

2013 Domestic	BSP MP's wife Jagriti Singh[44]	Maid Rakhi's death case: excessive beating and inhuman treatment, shoved iron clothes pin into victim's mouth	Husband's role in concealment of evidence, media and police pressure	Criminal arrested
2008 and 2013 Medical[45]	Multibillion, Gurgaon Kidney scandal (2008)	Poor patients from nearby western UP lured for Rs 30,000 per kidney removal or job opportunity. Kidneys were transplanted into foreign clients	Complaints by locals from Moradabad about illegal kidney sales	2013, CBI special court convicted five accused
Political 2013	Anti-corruption watchdog – The Transparency Bill, years of corruption	Eight unskilled attempts over the last five decades	Anna Hazare's[46] fasts, middle-class supporters, media activism	The Lokpal and Lokayukta Bill passed by voice vote
Political 2013	People voicing in India against corruption. Social movement (AAP), Anti-incumbency factor at Delhi Assembly Polls, 2013	Aggressive campaign to sweep off dishonest non-AAP parties	By AAP members and politically active middle-class supporters	Formation of AAP government in Delhi Assembly 2013,[47] changed political culture, increasing political socialization, rocking democracy, referendum to form coalition, direct democracy within indirect democracy

Cont'd...

...Cont'd

Media 2013	Mumbai photo[48] journalist case (interning in an English magazine)	Victim's colleague tied, crime in Shakti Mills compound	Silent protest by several journalist associations wearing black arm bands carrying placards 'city of shame'	Accused arrested
Religion and Media 2013	Allegations of self-shield Godman Asaram's tantric practices	Vaghela[49] case (death by two children)	1. Media, including women reporters beaten up	Kuldip Singh Kalair, a reporter with *Divya Bhaskar* locked up in a room and beaten by sadhaks
Media 2013	*Tehelka*[50] magazine's editor Tarun Tejpal	Tehelka's lady reporter	Media, gender activists and political parties	Arrest of the editor
		International Level		
2013 Domestic	Revealed in upcoming book of Obama's[51] brother Ndesandjo *An Obama's Journey: My Odyssey of Self-Discovery Across Three Cultures* Domestic Abuse of Obama Sr. (his father) to his mother	Describing alcohol fuelled beatings and holding knife to his mother's throat	Not welcomed by President's relatives for exposing private matters of family	His writings have alienated him from his family

Cont'd...

...Cont'd

2013 Diplomatic India-US	Diplomat Devyani Khobragade's[52] arrest	Handcuffed in public in New York on Visa fraud charges, treated like a common criminal	Displeasure by the leaders and officials of Indian Government, cancellation of meetings with US officials by Home Minister, Lok Sabha Speaker and National Security Advisor, respectively	United States agreed to shift her to its permanent UN mission, which will give her full diplomatic immunity from prosecution till she is in United States.
2013 Glamour world	Nina Davuluri[53] Miss America	First Indian American to hold the title	Racist comments on Twittersphere that displayed hate and linking her to terrorism	Unfortunately the same old racism
2010–2012 Child Labour	ILO[54] 'Accelerating Action Against Child Labour'	As many as 215 million children employed worldwide as child labourers; black money pool of 1,20,000 crores	United Nations (UN) and NGOs	Movement against child labour by ILO. Ratifications in ILO Convention Numbers 138 and 182
2014 ISIS[55]	Mass executions in the northern Iraqi city of Tikrit	Crimes against humanity, SAARC countries join fight against the ISIS	PM Narendra Modi in his UN speech includes India into fighting against terrorism	Jettisoned and signalled his support to the United States against terrorism.

transcends only castes that are being oppressed. The aforementioned examples best state that one both oppression and dominance are a natural phenomenon. Two, they originate within individuals vis-à-vis their action and speech. Three, it begins in a family which is the smallest unit, and then expands to various organizations. Four, at the largest level we have a level of dominance and oppression by sovereign nations vis-à-vis each other. Five, since it is 'natural', some remain suppressed and some dominant so this problem cannot be solved at the social, economic or political level (indicating difference between theory and practice) easily. Six, it may also be possible that an individual belonging to any caste, class, creed, race or sex may – at one level, with his relation to society at large – be suppressed and at another be an oppressor. Finally, this problem has a natural quality, which is found in an individual, who belongs to a family that has a natural origin; hence it is difficult to solve.

Coming back to the political level, the question is for how long the Dalit caste people could be suppressed by the upper castes. I discussed the Dalit movement till the pre-BSP phase. Can we relate the rise, decline and resurgence of the Dalit movement with any natural phenomenon? Since I have concluded above that to be a Dalit/grounded/oppressed or dominated is a natural quality of an individual. Then this quality should hold true for a group because it is the individuals who form the group and then the society, the political party and the state. The word natural has been used in the following senses:

natural quality (*Dalan*) of individual;
natural in the sense that individuals form family and family is natural as per its genesis;
Dalan by natural phenomena in environment;
change is the law of nature; and this process is also natural.

How any change in a political organization can have any similarities or dissimilarities with the natural environment?

Let us find out how the journey of the Dalit political party (twists and turns it took) was also natural? If yes, how? And to what extent? This answer leads us to the next chapter.

Notes

1. Norman Fairclough (2003). *Analysing Discourse: Textual Analysis for Social Research*. New York: Routledge. p. 51. Intertextuality means shaping of a text's meaning by another text. The term was coined by post-structuralist Julian Kristeva in 1966.
2. The French philosopher Jacques Derrida's theory of deconstruction. See *SEP* (*Stanford Encyclopedia of Philosophy*). First published 22 November 2006. Substantive revision. 3 June 2011.
3. Lene Hansen's (2011). 'Post structuralism', in *The Globalization of World Politics*, by John Baylis, Steve Smith and Patrica Owens. New York: Oxford. pp. 168–169.
4. Edith Hamilton and Huntington Cairns (eds.) (1961). *The Collected Dialogues of Plato*. Princeton: Princeton University Press. Also see Richard Krant (ed.) (1992). *The Cambridge Companion to Plato*. Cambridge: Cambridge University Press.
5. Susan Haslip (2003). 'Aristotle's Theory of the Good Life: A Consideration of the Role of Luck in Good Life and the Concept of Self-Sufficiency'. *Quodibet Journal*. 5(1). January.
6. Darrell Dobbs's (1996) 'Family Matters: Aristotle's Appreciation of Women and the Plural Structure of Society'. *American Political Science Review*. 90(1). p. 74.
7. P. Caws (ed.) (1989). *The Causes of Quarrel: Essays on Peace, War and Thomas Hobbes*. Boston: Beacon Press.
8. Peter Laslett (ed.) (1960). *Locke's Two Treaties of Government*. Cambridge. Cambridge University Press. Also see Richard Aschraft (ed.) (1989). *The Treaties of Civil Government*. London: Routledge.
9. R. Grimsley (1973). *The Philosophy of Rousseau*. Oxford: Oxford University Press. Also A. Bloom (1991). *Introduction to Rousseau*. J-J (1762). Emile. London: Penguin. J. Miller (1984). *Rousseau: Dreamer of Democracy*. London: Yale University Press.
10. Isaiah Berlin (1967). *Karl Marx: His Life and Environment*. New York: Time Inc. Book Division. p. 130. Also Alex Callinicos (1983). *The Revolutionary Ideas of Karl Marx*. Bloomsbury: London.

11. T. Bottomore (1993). *Elites and Society.* Second Edition. London: Routledge. Also see J. Burnham (1960). *The Managerial Revolution.* Bloomington: Indiana University Press.
12. Claudio Martinelli (2009). 'Gaetano Mosca's Political Theories: A Key to Interpret the Dynamics of Power'. *Italian Journal of Public Law.* Vol. I.
13. M. Seymour Lipset (1962). 'Introduction', in Robert Michels. *Political Parties: A Sociological Study of the Oligarchical Tendencies of Modern Democracy.* New York: Free Press, pp. 15–39.
14 Chandan Mukherjee, N. Krishnaji and Preet Rustogi. 'Crimes and Women in India'. *Economic and Political Weekly.* XXXVI(43). 27 October 2001.
15. Cecilia L. Ridgeway (2011). *Framed by Gender: How Gender Inequality Persists in the Modern World.* Oxford: Oxford University Press.
16. Ed Reep (2013). 'Men Are the Oppressed Gender'. *The Daily Targum.* 22 April. 12.00 am.
17. Bruce Hoffman (2006). *Inside Terrorism.* Second Edition. New York: Columbia University Press. Also Alex P. Schmid (ed.) (2011). *The Routledge Handbook of Terrorism Research.* New York: Routledge.
18. Nirvikar Singh (2010). 'The Trillion-Dollar Question'. *The Financial Express.* 19 December. Also 'India Corruption Study' (2008) Transparency International.
19. 'Baba Ramdev Meets PM Modi, Yoga Guru says 'Issues of National Importance Discussed' (2014). Zee Media Bureau. 4 November. 20.31 IST.
20. 'Black Money: Unhappy Anna Hazare Threatens Stir Against Centre'. (2014). bing.com/news. 28 October.
21. Zaheer Hasan (1986). *Gandhiji and Harijans.* Delhi. Shree. p. 63. Also T.K. Oomen (1990). *Protest and Change: Studies in Social Movement.* New Delhi: Sage. p. 261.
22. Thomas R. Shannon (1996). *An Introduction to the World-System Perspective.* Social Edition. Westview Press. ISBNO–8133–2452–1. pp. 94–95.
23. B.S. Murthy (1976). *Depressed and Oppressed (Forever in Agony).* Delhi: S. Chand. p. 179.

24. B.K. Ghatak (ed.) (1977). *Dr Ambedkar Thought*. Delhi: APH, p. 28.
25. 'Fight Must Be for Political Power' (2000). *The Pioneer*. 30 January. The New Millennium.
26. Thomas R. Shannon (1996). *An Introduction to the World System Perspective*. Second Edition. Colorado: Westview Press. pp. 94–95.
27. Paul James (1997). 'Post-Dependency: The Third World in an Era of Globalism and Late Capitalism'. *Alternatives: Social Transformation and Human Governance*. Vol. 22. 2 November. pp. 205–226. Also S. Amin (1976). 'Unequal Development: An Essay on the Social Formations of Peripheral Capitalism'. *New York Monthly Review Press.*
28. Manoj Joshi's (2013) article 'The Fumbling Soft State: Despite Its Size and Economy, India Looks Like a Pitiable Giant in Neighbourhood'. *Mail Today*. Delhi, 13 January, 15.48 IST.
29. Jacques E.C. Hymans (2010). 'India between "Soft State" and "Soft Power".' in *India in Transition* published by Center for the Advanced Study of India (CASI) of the University of Pennsylvania. 19 January.
30. 'India has 50 per cent of the World Modern Slaves'. *The Times of India*. 29 October 2013.
31. P. Michael Hanagan (1994). 'Class', in Peter N. Stearns *Encyclopedia of Social Theory*. Taylor and Francis. p. 184.
32. T. Bottomore (1993). *Elites and Society* (2nd ed.). London: Routledge. p. 59.
33. David Easton (1962). Introduction: The Current Meaning of 'Behaviouralism', in James Charlesworth (ed.). *Political Science*. Philadelphia: American Academy of Political and Social Science. Also Robert A. Dahl (1961). 'The Behavioural Approach in Political Science: Epitaph for a Monument to a Successful Protest'. *American Political Science Review*. December. 55(4). pp. 763–772.
34. Charles Handy (1993). *Understanding Organizations*. (4th ed.). London: Penguin.
35. Charles Lockhart (1993). 'Gabriel Almond', in *American Political Scientists: A Dictionary*. G. Utter and C. Lockhart (eds.). Greenwood Press.
36. Hannah Arendt (1961). *Between and Past and Future: The Concept of Authority*. New York: Viking.

37. Mattei Dogans (2003). 'Conceptions of Legitimacy', in Mary Hawkesworth and Maurice Kogan (eds.). (2003). *Encyclopedia of Government and Politics*. Second Edition. Vol. 2. London: Routledge. pp. 116–219.
38. Ben Wildavsky (2011). 'Academic Colonialism, False Consciousness and the Western University Ideal'. *The Chronicle of Higher Education*. 4 August.
39. Zee Media Bureau (2013). 'What Caused the Kedarnath Tragedy?' 20 June.13.05 IST.
40. 'Asaram Chhindwara Records Say Girl Is Minor: Police' (2013). *The Times of India*. 9 September.
41. 'Rare Pictures of Sex Assault Accused Narayan Sai' (2013). India TV Crime Desk. 24 October. 06:24:10 IST.
42. 'The Nirbhaya Case: Supreme Court Stays Death Sentence of Two Convicts' (2014). *The Hans India*. 14 July. 07.36 IST.
43. NDTV (2014). 8 January.
44. 'Maid Murder Case: Court Asks Tihar to Place Jagriti's Reports' (2014). Zee News. 9 October, 19.05 IST.
45. 'Five, Sentenced in Gurgaon Kidney Scam' (2013). *The Tribune*. 23 March. Chandigarh.
46. 'Anna Hazare to Fast at Relegan Sidhi for Jan Lok Pal Bill' (2013). Rediff.com News. 9 December. 13:19 IST.
47. 'Kejriwal Takes Oath as Delhi's Youngest CM'. (2013). *Yahoo India News*. 28 December.
48. 'Four Charged in Mumbai Photojournalist's Gangrape Case'. (2013). *The Times of India*. 19 September.
49. 'The Dark Side of Asaram Bapu' (2013). *Open*. 9 February.
50. 'Tarun Tejpal and Tehelka's Fall from Grace' (2013). *The Tribune*. 23 November.
51. 'Obama's Brother Writes about Domestic Abuse'. (2013). *The Times of India*. 20 December. p. 9.
52. 'Indian Official: Diplomat's Arrest in NYC Barbaric' (2013). Associated Press. 29 December.
53. 'American Beauty' (2013). *Sunday Times*. 22 September. p. 12.
54. 'Capital Corruption: Child Labour in India' (n.d.). *Bachpan Bachao Andolan*. Delhi.
55. Somini Sengupta and David E. Sanger (2014). *The New York Times*. 29 September. Huffington Post Politics (2014). More Countries Join Fight against ISIS (Reuters). 15 November.

4

The Eclipse Theory

Past to Post-Stage

Faith is the bird that feels the light
and sings when the dawn is still dark

—Rabindra Nath Tagore

For centuries, Dalit caste people were socially,[1] politically[2] and economically[3] deprived of their rights by the upper castes. If the former had any political clout and formed any political party on their own (as discussed in Chapter I), the movement petered out[4] due to various reasons – the main cause was their being co-opted by the 'upper-caste' parties.

But for how long can the same situation last? Change is the law of nature, as we all know.

This can be better explained diagrammatically as under (i, ii, iii, iv, v, vi) in Diagram I:

Though this is a political phenomenon that I have sought to explain for the convenience of readers, there can be a natural geographical phenomenon with which a parallel may be drawn in an interesting manner. This is a phenomenon of solar eclipse. As seen from the earth, it occurs when the moon passes between the sun and the earth and the moon fully or partially blocks the sun.[5]

The stages from BSP^{ii}, UCP^{ii} and BSP^{iii}, UCP^{iii} depict a case of beginning of decreasing PD leading to partial eclipse of BSP^{iv} and UCP^{iv} and further culminating in BSP^{v} and UCP^{v}, which is a phase of total eclipse. The UCP^{vi} and BSP^{vi} are post-eclipse stages. The 2014 Lok Sabha Poll results clearly

Diagram I

Eclipse Theory

Political Position of BSP vis-à-vis Political Structure in Various Phases

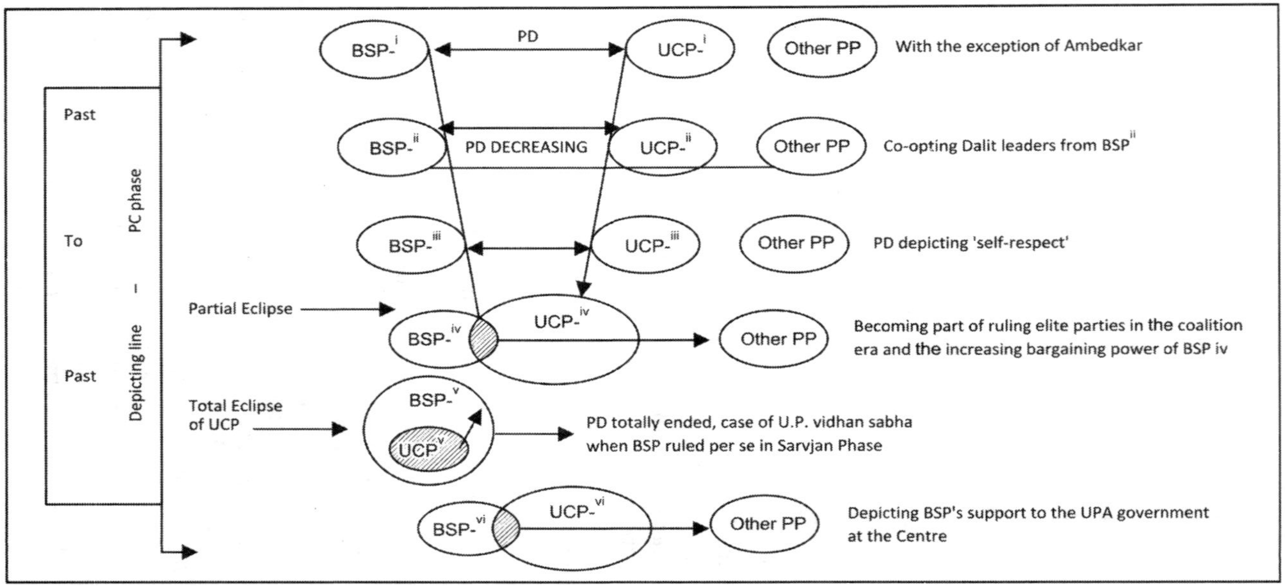

(i to vi) Depicting phases; PP → Political Parties; BSP → Bahujan Samaj Party; UCP → Upper Caste Parties; PD → Political Distance between Parties. Bigger circle → Shows increase in numbers; PC phase shows post-colonial phase.

reveal total eclipse of BSP^{vi} by the UCP (BJP) where the BSP seats were totally zeroed down. The space gap from BSP^{1} and UCP^{1} to BSP^{v} and UCP^{v} can be compared to the distance of $(UCP)_{Sun}$, $(other\ PP)_{earth}$ and $(BSP)_{moon}$. Though this comparison may invoke derision of my critics, yet I wish to make my readers understand only one point through this similie. Before detailed analyses of the diagram, it would be prudent to conclude if we can apply this eclipse theory to any other political phenomenon? If yes, how? The following diagram amply depicts the aforementioned theory.

Diagram II

Application of the Eclipse Theory

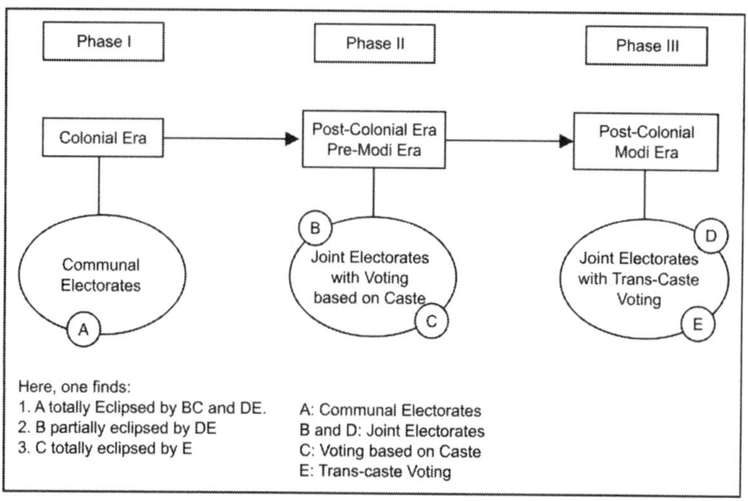

In Diagram I, we know through the centuries that the Dalit caste was hated[6] and looked down upon and was meant to do menial tasks.[7] Its shadows were considered polluted, and one could never imagine a low-caste Dalit leader, – a woman – could become the fountainhead of power in Uttar Pradesh[8] with a lot of bargaining power with the coalition government at the centre. It explains how the once powerless could become powerful through the (PC, PD) distance of time (as discussed further).

The fact is that an eclipse occurs every year but Dalits had to cover a distance of centuries to attain political equality.[9] The 'social'[10] and 'economic' equality[11] lags vis-à-vis upper-caste people still continues to dominate.

The phase from BSP^{i} vis-à-vis UCP^{i} to BSP^{iv}-UCP^{iv} has already been discussed at length in Chapter I. Let us find out how the Bahujan Samaj Party (BSP) grew within a short time into a national party. And did the party in any of its electoral strategies transcend beyond the boundaries of caste to woo the voters? If yes, how? Was it able to do something substantial to uplift Dalits? Or it is a bitter truth that the Dalit politicians have done little for the economic and social upliftment of their brethren?

It is both interesting and necessary to focus here on the BSP supremo,[12] Kanshi Ram's (a Sikh Chamar from Ropar, Punjab)[13] perception about the failure[14] in any of the efforts made for solving problem of Dalits by social or political reformers and leaders, state's legislative measures,[15] political parties,[16] Backward class movements[17] and also the Dalit movements of the past.

Kanshi Ram considered Gandhi as the custodian of the status quo. Gandhi wanted shudras to remain shudras.[18] He said, 'we are working to unite the nation and erase all artificial divisions'. The Congress Party has been, Kanshi Ram declared, drawing upon Ambedkar's description of it as a unique blend of 'capitalism' and 'brahmanism'.[19] It is a 'Manuwadi' and 'brahmanical' party. It is because of this attitude that benefits have not trickled down to the weaker sections despite significant programmes for the latter. Disgusted with the effort of communists and describing them as 'green snakes in green grass', he said they do not work for change.[20] Even the backward caste movement headed by V.P. Singh (messiah) whom he (Kanshi Ram) considered as a 'first-class hypocrite', had not worked for Dalits.[21]

The BSP, in particular, held the view that no genuine attempt has been made in the past for socio-economic and political upliftment of hitherto marginalized classes.

It is pertinent here to accept that BSP did fill up the space (if not vacuum) created by the decline (and exhaustion) of the

Ambedkarite groups and the landslide of the all pervasive Congress system.[22] Noticeable in the 1960s were the mass movement under the leadership of Charan Singh[23] and Ram Manohar Lohia. In the later decade, they made impact on the national political canvass. Meanwhile the new class – OBCs (other backward castes) and MBCs (most backward castes) – became a new class of beneficiaries through the implementation of the Mandal Commission Report.[24] This phase made it possible for the BSP to make a special representation of more castes with the idea of floating the word 'Bahujan'[25] – Dalits plus OBCs. Uneducated rural youth also felt attracted to the BSP. With this, the BSP found a new opportunity to broad base its electoral strength.[26]

There was a delayed political mobilization of Dalits in Uttar Pradesh as compared to Maharashtra.[27] The Dalit movement of the BSP has been described as a part of the New Social Movements (NSMs).

The BSP has its origin in a lower-middle-class 'trade union' organization of government employees – the BAMCEF[28] (Backward and Minorities Community Employees Federation) founded in 1976 by the late Kanshi Ram. It was formed to find solution to the harassment of employees and had established its office in New Delhi. It created the terminology of 'Man, money and mind power'[29] to depict the future of its movement and an important programme was 'Ambedkar Mela on Wheels'. It was based on the motto: 'Educate, organise and agitate' (adopted from Ambedkar).

In 1981, Kanshi Ram replaced it with DS–4[30] (Dalit Samaj Shoshit Sangharsh Samiti), which was a quasi-political party. Its main popular programme was 'Miracle of two feet and two wheels',[31] and 'Peoples' Parliament'. The popular slogan it carried forward was 'Brahman, Thakur, Bania Chor, Baki *Sab hein* DS–4'.[32]

The groundwork done by Kanshi Ram – through BAMCEF, DS–4 and media *The Oppressed Indian*, *Bahujan Times* and *Bahujan Sangthak*[33], gave him ample mass-base to launch a full-fledged political party[34] (14 April 1984) on Baba Saheb Bhimrao Ambedkar's 85th birth anniversary.

Thus in 1980s it was the only non-upper-caste party in UP with the object of alleviating the plight of Dalits.[35] The party adopted RPI's election symbol – an elephant. Its blue flag depicted struggle against injustice. It popularized a few couplets:

BSP Ki Kya Pahchan,
Neela Jhanda Hathi Nishan,
Chalega Hathi, Udegi Dhool,
Na Rahega Panja, Na Rahega Phool;
'Jaisa To Taisa', Jo Daliton Se
Takaraiga, mitti me mil jaiga[36]

These clearly depict an agitational language with which they address the 'Manuwadi' politics. The BSP co-workers greet each other by saying 'Jai Bhim,[37] Jai Bharat'.

Other slogans of the BSP include *Mat hamara, raj tumhara, nahin chalega nahi chalega;*[38] *Vote se lenge PM, CM, arakshan se SP/DM;*[39] *Tilak, taraju aur talwar.*[40]

The central tenet of its ideology is the concept of 'social justice' that is too retributive to strive for establishing a new social and political order. Kanshi Ram was interested in power movement with the ultimate aim to rule India. Political power is the key by which any lock could be opened.[41] For this Kanshi Ram showed strict adherence to the constitution and parliamentary democracy throughout his struggle which brings him closer to Ambedkar.

The BSP duo felt that 'If the social and economic inequalities are not done away with, the victims of this inequality will pull down the edifice of democracy'.[42] The latter means rule of the majority, which comprises the Scheduled Castes, Scheduled Tribes and other backward castes and religious minorities.

Mayawati firmly believes that political reform[43] and social reform are two wheels of the same vehicle and absence of any one of them would bring the vehicle to a grinding halt. Kanshi Ram's message – *Jati toro (thodo), samaj joro*[44] *(jodo)* – was to unite society by demolishing caste.

Aforementioned discussion points to two factors: one, how the BSP will play the caste card to woo voters; and two what efforts have been made by the BSP to demolish the caste system.

Kanshi Ram borrowed heavily from Phule's thesis of Bahujan Samaj.[45] Bahujan, according to Kanshi Ram, consisted of SCs, STs, OBCs and converted minority people, and bahujan was used as an electoral strategy.

For Kanshi Ram, self-respect and dignity were as important as political empowerment of the Dalits. He preferred social transformation to social change.[46] He felt that the issue of reservation is akin to clutches. He wanted to build a kind of social and political structure in which Brahmans could be given reservation in proportion to their own meagre population. The BSP duo preferred unstable governments as they felt each election would enhance 'Dalit Consciousness' in the mind of its voters.[47]

A number of symbols, which are an integral part of the Dalit movement of Maharashtra, made their way into the socio-political field of UP during Mayawati's tenure as the chief minister (in the past).[48] Likewise Shahuji Maharaj and Mahatma Phule were projected as 'Kurmi' and 'Mali' caste leaders.

During its term of governance the BSP attempted to highlight those great personalities, who took up the cause of Dalits in fields of politics, religion, social reform and warfare.[49] Lord Buddha and his mother Mahamaya, Sant Ravidas and Mahatma Jyotiba Phule, Chhatarpati Shahuji Maharaj and Ahilya Bai Holkar, and Rani Laxmibai and Halkaribai were sought to be commemorated[50] by the creation of new 'chowks', districts and parks and holding 'melas' after their names[51] (in UP). Awards were also instituted in the memory of champions of social change.

Another important part of the programme was to fund those villages with Dalit population of 30 per cent for building the infrastructure under the Ambedkar village scheme.[52] Brahman officials were transferred and replaced by Dalit officers in various political and administrative positions.[53] Also, a special drive was launched against criminals to end the *jungle raj*. At the state level, women's[54] committee was constituted for protection of their rights.

My aim is to discuss the BSP and its ideology/programme in brief and later its strategies to decipher and make an in-depth analysis as to whether the BSP understood Dalit only in the caste sense or in a broader perspective (as discussed in Chapter

3) that is, class, gender also. Though, of course, prima facie it talks of Dalit only in the caste sense.

It was due to the aforementioned tactics that the BSP was successful in creating political awareness among the SCs who came up in large numbers to exercise their vote.[55] So there was a steady rise in SC voter turnout. The use of anti-upper-caste slogans by the BSP duo created self-confidence among Dalits. An important electoral strategy was *Jiski Jitni Sankhya Bhari, Utni uski bhagidari* meaning the choice of a candidate be determined by the numerical strength of caste in any constituency.[56] Apart from Dalits and backward castes, it nominated Muslims and upper-caste candidates, with a view to consolidating BSP's political base.[57] Its top leaders preferred to enter into alliances, regardless of ideological differences,[58] with other contesting political parties – a la striking an alliance with Samajwadi Party (SP), forming a pre-election alliance with the Congress, allying afresh with Bharatiya Janata Party (BJP). The motive was to stop the loot of Dalit votes.[59] Apart from improving its strength in the UP legislature (by forming a government per se under Mayawati's chief ministership), the BSP improved its strength in the Lok Sabha too and emerged as a 'balancing' or 'deciding' factor to make or break a ministry.[60]

BSP's main focus has been to cater to the group needs to create an identity – like a small section of Dalits in eastern UP vis-à-vis the upper-middle-castes in the western counterpart. BSP also received support of Kurmis (OBCs) – being political orphans – both in eastern and western sectors.[61] The BSP managed to please them by giving them tickets.

The above discussion pinpoints many factors. Here, I am analysing again to understand the Dalit meaning in a broader sense, especially with reference to BSP's politics. First, in the pre-bahujan phase, one finds BSP clinging to pro-Dalit approach, which clearly indicates that the term Dalit was used as an electoral tool, only in the 'caste' sense. Second, in the Bahujan phase, for the first time, the party broadened its vision beyond the exclusive interests of Dalits to include the BCs. The pertinent point that cannot be ignored here is though trans-caste 'Dalit' strategy was used to cling to power (coalition with SP), the stark reality, that led to the downfall of the government in UP, was (besides other factors) Mayawati's catering to pro-Dalit hard line politics, which invited the wrath of BCs.

Third, the BJP-BSP experiment also failed due to various reasons and the main issue leading to differences was that the BSP felt that BJP's (coalition parties) politics was not Dalit oriented. This clearly shows that at the post-bahujan phase, BSP was clinging to 'Manuwadi' party – BJP – to remain in power. Fourth, though BSP's initial slogans were totally pro-Dalit, but later on distributing tickets to upper castes and allying with 'Manuwadi' parties' depicts its change in understanding the idea of the Dalit factor from the caste to the inter-caste.

Fifth, the formation of women's committee by the BSP for protection of women's rights indicates the broader understanding of the word Dalit not only in the caste but in the gender sense as well. And finally, the Sarvjan phase – an electoral tool used by the BSP to woo the upper castes' votes by distributing tickets to them as well as to the MBCs (Most Backward Castes) – shows that the word Dalit is used in the class sense here.

The idea to discuss the BSP's genesis, ideology, alliances and strategies (in short) was just to decipher whether the party talks of definition of Dalit only on caste lines (in theory) or has it transcended this factor for its political gains (in practice).

Hence, my paradigm vis-à-vis Dalit-caste to understand the term Dalit in a holistic manner is summarized in the next chapter.

Notes

1. T.K. Oomen (2000). 'Contours of Mind'. *The Pioneer*. 30 January.
2. Nicholas B. Dirks (2001). *Castes of Mind*. Princeton: Princeton University Press. p. 3.
3. M.S.S. Pandhian (2002). 'One Step Outside Modernity'. *Economic and Political Weekly*. XXXVII(18). 4–10 May. pp. 173536. Also Gail Omvedt (1999). 'Dalits and Elections I'. *The Hindu*. 5 November.

4. Oven M. Lynch (1974). *The Politics of Unouchability.* Delhi: National Publishing House. p. 66. Also C.P. Bhambhri (1999). 'Dialectics of Caste and Casteism'. *Economic and Political Weekly.* XXXIV(36). 4 September. p. 2619. Lata Murugkar (1991). *Dalit Panther Movement in Maharashtra (A Sociological Appraisal).* Bombay: Bombay Popular Prakashan. p. 236.
5. Littmann, Mark, Espenak, Fred, and Willox, Ken (2008). *Totality: Eclipses of the Sun.* Oxford: Oxford University Press. pp. 18–19.
6. T.K. Oomen (1999). 'Dalit and Production of Knowledge I'. *The Hindu.* 13 September.
7. Sukhadeo Thorat (2002). 'Oppression and Denial: Dalit Discrimination in the 1990s'. *Economic and Political Weekly.* XXXVII(6). 9 February. p. 572.
8. Zoya Hasan (2001). 'Transfer of Power? Politics of Mass Mobilization in UP'. *Economic and Political Weekly.* XXXVI(46/47). 24–30 November. p. 4405.
9. Kanshi Ram (n.d.). 'Swatantra Bharat Mein Bahujan Samaj Ashrit Kyon?' BSP Party Pamphlet. Also S.K. Thorat and R.K. Deshpande (2001). 'Caste System and Economic Inequality', in Ghanshyam Shah (ed.). *Dalit Identity and Politics.* Delhi: Sage. p. 69.
10. Hiranmay Dhar (1992). 'Escalating Violence on Harijans'. *Economic and Political Weekly.* XXXVII(38). 19 September. p. 1300. Also Uday Mehta (1998). 'Social Transformation in India'. *One India, One People.* Vol. 2/3. October. p. 18. Vasanthi Devi (2000). 'Dalits and the State'. *Frontline.* 21 July. pp. 22–25.
11. 'Fight Must Be for Political Power' (2000). *The Pioneer.* 30 January. The New Millennium.
12. Gail Omvedt (1994). 'Kanshi Ram and the BSP', in K.L. Sharma (ed.). *Caste and Class in India.* Jaipur: Rawat Publications. p. 163.
13. *The Tribune* (1994). 6 May.
14. Lancy Lobo (2001). 'Vision, Illusions and Dilemmas of Dalit Christians', in Ghanshyam Shah (ed.). *Dalit Identity and Politics.* Delhi: Sage. p. 243. Also Koennad Elst (1993). *Dr Ambedkar: A True Aryan.* Delhi: Voice of India. p. 4.

15. Sukhadeo Thorat (2002). 'Oppression and Denial: Dalit Discrimination in the 1990s'. *Economic and Political Weekly*. XXXVII(6). 9 February. p. 578.
16. Vivek Kumar (2001). 'Political Utility of Dalits'. *The Pioneer*. 15 February. Editor Page. Also Rajni Kothari (1994). 'Rise of Dalits and the Renewed Debate on Caste'. *Economic and Political Weekly*. XXIX(26). 25 June. p. 1593.
17. *The Sunday Observer* (1990). 12 August.
18. *The Illustrated Weekly of India* (1987), 8 March, quoted in Ambeth Rajan's (1994), *My Bahujan Samaj Party*. New Delhi: ABCDE Publications. p. 38.
19. Sudha Pai (1998). 'The BSP in UP'. *Seminar* 471. November. pp. 207–210.
20. Kancha Ilaiah (2001). 'Dalitism versus Brahminism: The Epistemological Conflict in History', in Ghanshyam Shah (ed.) *Dalit Identity and Politics*. New Delhi: Sage. p. 107.
21. *The Sunday Observer* (1990). 12 August.
22. Oliver Mendelson and Marika Vicziany (2000). *The Untouchables*. Delhi: Cambridge University Press. pp. 207–209.
23. T.J. Byres (1988). 'Charan Singh (1902–1987): An Assessment'. *Journal of Peasant Studies (JPS)*. 15(2). Also Craig Jeffrey (2000). 'Democratization without Representation'. *Political Geography*. 19(8). November. p. 1015.
24. Gail Omvedt (2000). 'The Purpose of Reservation I'. *The Hindu*. 24 March.
25. Ravindra K. Jain (1996). 'Hierarchy, Hegemony and Dominance'. *Economic and Political Weekly*. 27 January. p. 215.
26. Pradeep Kumar (1999). 'Bahujan Samaj Party Breaking Ground Realities in Uttar Pradesh II'. *Mainstream*. 8 May, p. 21.
27. Jim Masselos (1983). 'Jobs and Jobbery: The Sweeper in Bombay under Raj'. *The Indian Economic and Social History Review*. 19(2). pp. 101–135. Also Yurlova Yevgenia (1991). 'Political Emergence of the Ethno Community'. *Mainstream*. XXXIX(51). 12 October. p. 21.
28. Sudha Pai (1999). *State Politics: New Dimensions*. New Delhi: Shipra. p. 118.

29. Vivek Kumar and Uday Sinha (2001). *Dalit Assertion and Bahujan Samaj Party: A Perspective from Below.* Lucknow: Bahujan Samaj Party Publishers. p. 60.
30. Barbara R. Joshi (1986). *Untouchable: Voice of Dalit Liberation Movement.* New Delhi: Select Book Service Syndicates. p. 111.
31. Started on 15 March 1983.
32. Shaibal Gupta (1998). 'From Untouchable to Dalit'. *Biblio: A Review of Books.* III(11/12). November–December. p. 6. (Book Review).
33. Vivek Kumar and Uday Sinha (2001). *Dalit Assertion and Bahujan Samaj Party: A Perspective from Below.* Lucknow: Bahujan Samaj Party Publishers. p. 62.
34. Udit Raj (2002). 'An Unholy Alliance'. *Indian Express.* 6 May.
35. Sudha Pai (2001). 'The State, Social Justice and Dalit Movement: The BSP in UP', in Nirja Gopal Jayal and Sudha Pai (eds.). *Democratic Governance in India.* New Delhi: Sage. p. 202.
36. It expresses its (BSP's) views regarding the symbols of both the Congress and the BJP. The Dalits, who have in the past all along been crushed under the feet of the Congress and the BJP, will no longer remain exploited once the BSP attains political power.
37. Meaning victory to Bhim, shortening of Ambedkar's first name, Bhimrao.
38. Translation: 'We Vote, you You Rule'. This cannot go on. Tulsi Ram (1999). 'Antim Daav Hein Rajneetic Asthirtha'. *Rashtriya Sahara.* 4 September. (Hindi). Mahesh Rangarajan (1999). 'The BSP: Dalit Power of the Force'. *The Times of India.* 20 August.
39. Translation: 'Through the vote we will take the posts of Prime Minister and Chief Minister and through reservation we will take posts of Superintendent of Police and District Magistrate'. For Further details see Radhika Ramaseshan (1995). 'Dalit Politics in UP'. *Seminar* (425). January. p. 73.
40. Tulsi Ram (1999). 'Antim Daav Hein Rajneetic Asthirtha'. *Rashtriya Sahara.* 4 September (Hindi).
41. P.S. Verma (2001). 'Dalit Mobilization in Punjab'. Paper (abstract) presented in a seminar, Panjab University, Chandigarh. 27–28 February.

42. Mayawati (2000). 'Bahujan Samaj Aur Uski Rajneeti'. Delhi. Bahujan Samaj Party (Published by). pp. Introduction, 31, 79.
43. Gail Omvedt (1999). 'Dalits and Elections II'. *The Hindu*. 6 January.
44. Quoted in Ambeth Rajan (1994). *My Bahujan Samaj Party*. New Delhi. ABCDE Publications. pp. 32, 55, 56.
45. Sudha Pai's article (2001). 'The State Social Justice and Dalit Movement, The BSP in UP', in Nirja Gopal Jayal and Sudha Pai (ed.). *Democratic Governance in India*. New Delhi: Sage. p. 296.
46. Radhika Ramaseshan (1995). 'Dalit Politics in UP'. *Seminar 425*. January. p. 73.
47. Ambeth Rajan (1994). *My Bahujan Samaj Party*. New Delhi: ABCDE Publications. p. 105.
48. Mayawati (2000), 'Bahujan Samaj Aur Uski Rajneeti'. Delhi: Bahujan Samaj Party (published by). p. 92.
49. Mohammad Jamil Akhtar (1999). *Iron Lady*. New Delhi: Bahujan Sangthak. pp. 111–116.
50. 'Naye Samaj Ki Oor' (1997). Lucknow. Information and Public Relations. 8 July. pp. 8–9.
51. Pradeep Kumar (1999). 'Dalits and the BSP in UP'. *Economic and Political Weekly*. 3 April. p. 822.
52. Mohammad Jamil Akhtar (1999). *Iron Lady*. New Delhi. Bahujan Sangathak. p. 89.
53. Sudha Pai (2001). 'The State, Social Justice, Politics and Dalit Movement: The BSP in UP', in Nirja Gopal Jayal and Sudha Pai (eds.) (2001). *Democratic Governance in India*. New Delhi: Sage. p. 216.
54. 'Kalyan and Vikas Yojna' (n.d.). Lucknow. Minority Welfare and Waqf Department. p. 49.
55. Amaresh Mishra (1998). 'UP Order Behind Anarchy'. *Economic and Political Weekly*. XXXIII(18). 2 May. p. 4011.
56. Abhay Kumar Dubey (2001). 'Anatomy of Dalit Power Player: A Study of Kanshi Ram', in Ghanshyam Shah (ed.). *Dalit Identity and Politics*. Delhi: Sage. p. 297.
57. Mohammad Jamil Akhtar (1999). *Iron Lady*. New Delhi: Bahujan Sangathak. pp. 13–34, 133.

58. Vivek Kumar and Uday Sinha (2001). *Dalit Assertion and Bahujan Samaj Party: A Perspective from Below.* Lucknow: Bahujan Samaj Party Publishers. p. 74.
59. Pradeep Kumar (1998). 'Understanding Strategies – The Bahujan Samaj Party'. *Politics India.* June. pp. 19–25.
60. It helped to defeat the Vajpayee Government.
61. Sudha Pai (2002). Dalit Assertion and Unfinished Democratic Revolution: The Bahujan Samaj Party in Uttar Pradesh. New Delhi: Sage. p. 153.

5

Conclusions and Suggestions

Dalit political movement in India preceding the attainment of freedom on 15 August 1947 began as a social movement and later culminated into a political one. Its colonial stage saw the support from *dwija*, *non-dwija* leaders, poets, writers, British rulers and Congress Party for eradication of the pricky problem of untouchability. The first chapter has sought to elucidate the concept of Dalit Movement (DM), tracing its genesis and relating it to Dalit politics. The changes, vis-à-vis the social status of Dalits that took place, albeit slow, were enormous. It answered many questions à la about the efforts to educate, politicize and raise Dalit Consciousness (DC) through intellectual activity. It was just when independent India included Article 17 in the Indian Constitution, with the efforts of our first (Dalit) Law Minister Dr B.R. Ambedkar – the mere execution of the law produced high expectations in Dalits vis-à-vis their social status. The chapter includes oft erupted DMs – both social and political – in south and west India, interrupted by failures as discussed. Due to the subsequent breakdown of DMs, Dalit Panthers (DP), Independent Labour Party (ILP), Scheduled Caste Federation (SCF) and RPI (Republican Party of India) – the euphoria with which Dalits greeted it was later dissipated to a large extent. Yet Dalits earned a relatively better position as compared to their dark past. This chapter surveys and analyses the social, historical, political and intellectual forces that led to various DMs in different parts of India.

The second chapter gives an analytical description of the various synonyms used for the term Dalit from the pre-colonial to the colonial and the post-colonial era. It shows how the word was given a different meaning not only by different leaders, *dwija* and non-*dwija*, but also by the British rulers. It analyses the nature of DM as an evolutionary one. It introduces a main thought and attempts to throw light on neo-caste, post-structure and realist theories. This neo-position forces us to rethink our old concept of social stratification. It provides an alternative approach to the older one by giving the social problem a new philosophical outlook, based on empiricism (as depicted in Tables III to V in Chapters 2 and 3).

The neo-caste theory gives an ethical colour to the caste issue – one of the biggest challenges India faces today. In order to evaluate further the meaning of Dalit, Chapter 3 is a modest attempt at a new philosophical understanding of the term.

The term Dalit – as always, related to caste – has been analysed philosophically, and examples of *Dalan*/Dalit/being grounded have been explained in a trans-caste sense by analysing the theories of various political thinkers, thereby making it (Dalit) a very fluid concept. The chapter attempts to treat the word Dalit (largely understood) from caste perspective in a trans-caste way. From the most particularistic to the most generalistic way, how it can be evaluated and understood has been given with examples. And these (except for the hypothetical theoretical formation of political philosophers) are based on universal truths. It is possible to argue that Dalit/*Dalan* can simply be experienced within an individual, in relation to individual, groups of all kinds vis-à-vis actions relating to self and to others as per the goals that need to be achieved. And this also holds true for a nation's policy-making (at international level), which includes colonialism practiced by the British in the past, understanding of the centre-periphery model in the contemporary era and why India came to be known as 'soft state' vis-à-vis its neighbouring states. This may not alter our dominant understanding of the word Dalit denoting lowest caste. But the new form of Dalit-understanding (based on concept of nature and natural) as discussed can be added, meaning thereby to be Dalit/oppressed or dominated at any level in any system or structure is a natural quality of an individual (as concluded and explained in Chapter 3).

When we talk of Dalit, the genesis of Bahujan Samaj Party (BSP) cannot be ignored (dealt in Chapter 4). It focuses on Dalit politics in contemporary India. The Dalit parties of the past and the BSP have been described through eclipse theory (borrowed from Geography). The advent of BSP in UP (Uttar Pradesh) marked the beginning of Dalits becoming a decisive political force in Indian politics. The autonomous working of BSP on various strategies for forming a support base, both caste and region-wise, indicated that it was a result of democratic concept arising from exclusivist politics. That is one reason why it decided to expand its ideology from *bahujan* to *sarvjan*. The idea to study BSP here is (i) it is based on Dalit politics, and (ii) to evaluate whether it transcended the caste factor and used it as a political tool to woo voters. In the second chapter, I have, especially, mentioned the problem of scavenging. I have, particularly, discussed only this issue as it is the most hated form of menial work carried out by Dalits even today. Through many ideologies and party programmes of BSP that have been discussed in the last chapter, it is clear that no effort was ever made by the BSP to solve this huge problem. Though BSP has achieved the goal of political equality, the perennial problems of social and economic inequality still remain.

To pinpoint a few crucial questions to our readers, that is, in this era of post-modernism, can we find a Dalit (scholar in Sanskrit, with knowledge of Shastras) heading a temple in India? Will it be acceptable to upper-castes and also lower-caste people? After all, how can the mindset be changed? If by deleting surnames for another 200 years by everyone, social egalitarianism can be brought about, then where is the political will of both BSP and 'Manuwadi' parties? In fact, in India discrimination and *Dalan*/oppression (caste sense) is executed where its meant for political gains and not used where not necessary. If we relate Dalit caste factor to medical department, the core question will be why is it that blood or organ donors' castes remain anonymous and why is there no discrimination on the basis of caste vis-à-vis organ transplantation and blood transfusion for the upper castes? This also holds true in cases of surrogacy and adoption of children when the latter's caste is not given any importance.

Such questions may raise eyebrows but remain unsolved despite political equality achieved by the BSP today.

The main focus in all chapters is to give a 'holistic picture of the term Dalit'. The discussion can be summarized as Dalit (to be oppressed) is a habit of the soul, the mind and the heart, which exists in every individual. It is a natural quality of all individuals vis-à-vis others. It is found in caste, class and all kinds of groups. To understand further, the examples are Dalit-caste, Dalit-class, Dalit-social and economic and political group. This Dalit/*Dalan* has to be understood both at intra- and inter-group levels. So, from the individual's soul to the level of the nation, it can be understood (as discussed). Its new meaning introduces a way to structure Dalit (as given diagrammatically) and theorize it in new ways. Using a number of different concepts, approaches and realist-caste and eclipse theories thus introduced, some other ways to understand Dalit structure ipso facto, and not always in relation to caste as it always is explained.

So this holistic approach leads to change in our perception (in a more particularistic and more generalistic manner). At the heart of the new paradigm of Dalit includes queries such as what are the new challenges if the word is so understood? At the level of caste, the problem can be solved by our polity if not today, then in the coming years. But if we understand it as quality/habit of heart and mind of the individual, the crux is the oppression, and domination will be difficult to solve as it results from an individual's nature and is a natural quality which holds universal truth. This will remain true for all groups beginning from the family and ending at the state as it is the individuals (natural beings) who make the society and the state.

The trans-caste model, if applied to the current situation in all societies, reveals that if various types of *Dalan* are ignored by the welfare state, the aggravated situation will lead to deep crises in legitimacy. This, in turn, will adversely affect the persistence of the political system, leading to anarchy and, in worst situations, lead to bloody revolution in any state. The civil movements in India and abroad are recent examples of this situation. We witnessed how citizens' activism was born in India through the street protestations and, in a way, this activism not only curbed *Dalan* but also improved political socialization and participation to a great extent.

This neo-understanding will help analyse stability, change and development in all societies. In short, the understanding of Dalit is a complex, hybrid phenomenon in which both groups and the state share a host of responsibilities to run amicably. But the role of the state and groups comes later. The right kind of socialization in family, solution of intra-family *Dalan* caused by own blood relations by making moral rights justiciable, introduction of moral courts for the same, is the need of the hour (as moral values have degraded).

The questions to ponder are (i) family, as we all know, is the smallest unit of society where the right kind of socialization is essential to produce good citizens who, in turn, are a part of the state. It is the good citizens (whether governing or non-governing) who can help make good governance successful. Good rulers will, in Aristotelian sense, run a normal (and not a perverted government – be it of any type). And the good ruled would be active citizens who will be vigilant enough and will try to curb *Dalan* by the rulers or other systems. (ii) For pursuing education and career, nuclear family is also breaking down now. In most cases, we see teenaged children leaving homes and living alone for pursuing career or jobs. In such a situation, which has led to withering away of the nuclear family, will the primary source (family) be contained at a later stage by secondary agencies of socialization? Can an individual learn better moral values outside the family or within the family? Is it that probability of being misguided outside the family increases in an impressionable age? The answer may be positive or negative. If it is the latter, then will this have an adverse effect on his/her behaviour in society, vis-à-vis others, as an oppressor/oppressed that can take any form of *Dalan*?

The broader problem of *Dalan* and Dalits, as discussed, may be solved when Lumenosophy will trickle down in the conscience of the family, the community and the state. It would be akin to Lumenarchy in Skolimowskian terms. Only when democracy along with cosmocracy, 'conscious parenting', introduction of new subject on gender respect at school level will usher in, that we can have a new era of egalitarianism and happiness that will curb and contain *Dalan* and solve problems of Dalits in the universe forever. This is just a semi-idealistic solution. More important and practical approach is when both intra- and international governments will understand the various causes of *Dalan* and frame laws or policies accordingly. Such problems should also be taken up seriously by the UN members.

In the preceding chapters, we have understood how the flow and fall of the river of *Dalan* is tumultuous. It integrates and diverges its course in various systems. It would be interesting to note that the modernity of tradition (caste) is taking newer shapes, not only as trans-caste *Dalan* but also as trans-caste occupation, voting and the latest being the cleanliness (Swatchata) drive in India. The implementation of the drive with a broomstick in the hands of several volunteers is path-breaking, inspiring and help understand the trans-caste phenomenon. It is two-pronged strategy. One, as is prima facie sweep to clean environment and two, sweep to clean the mindset, vis-à-vis caste to bring about an egalitarian set-up, which may facilitate to end trans-caste *Dalan* in social, political and economic set-up of our society. The new trans-caste idiom of caste thus becomes an important area of study.

> This, however, does not mean that our old understanding of the term has become outdated or redundant.
>
> All doctrines are right in their own respective spheres – but if they encroach upon the province of doctrines and try to refute their views, they are wrong.
>
> —Sanmatitarka of Siddhasena 1.28

Although our old mindset, vis-à-vis caste, persists, yet new paradigm, prism and perceptions will hopefully trigger a new debate in the not too distant future.

Glossary

Absolute Sovereignty: A state has ultimate law making authority over a given territory.

Asphyxiation: This is a word for dying from lack of oxygen. A condition arising when the body is deprived of oxygen, causing unconsciousness or death

Authority: The power to enforce laws, exact obedience, command, determine or judge.

Bourgeoisie: Class that own means of production.

Brahmanism: An early religion of Indian subcontinent.

Capitalism: An economic system characterized by private or corporate ownership of capital assets and goods.

Center-Periphery Model: One in which authority is concentrated in a single centre which is more or less influenced by its periphery, depending upon the situation in which it finds itself. The centre-periphery (or core-periphery) model is a spatial metaphor that describes and attempts to explain the structural relationship between the advanced or metropolitan 'centric' and a less developed 'periphery', either within a particular country or (more commonly) as applied to the relationship between capitalist and developing societies.

Concept: A general idea derived or inferred from specific instances or occurrences. Something formed in the mind, a thought or notion.

Dalan: It is referring to ground down to pieces like grinding grain ('daal').

Dalit: It is a designation for group of traditionally regarded as untouchable. Dalits are a mixed population consisting of numerous social groups from all over India; they speak a variety of languages and practice a multitude of religions.

Dalit-Panther: It is a social organization founded by Namdev Dhasal in April 1972 in Mumbai. Later many Dalit activists joined this organization.

Dalitwa: It means dalitness or untouchability.

Deconstruction: It is a form of philosophical and literary analysis, derived mainly from work in the 1960s by the French philosopher Jacques Derrida. It is analytic examination of something (as a theory) often in order to reveal its inadequacy.

Depressed Classes: During the period of British rule in the Indian subcontinent, the Scheduled Castes and Scheduled Tribes were known as the depressed classes.

Doctrine: (from Latin: *doctrina*) is a codification of beliefs or body of teachings or instructions, taught principles or positions, as the body of teachings in a branch of knowledge or belief system.

Empirical: Relying on a derived from observation or experiment.

Epistemology: It is the branch of philosophy concerned with the nature and scope of knowledge and is also referred to as 'theory of knowledge'. It questions what knowledge is and how it can be acquired and the extent to which any given subject or entity can be known.

Evolution (social): The gradual development of society and social forms, institutions, etc. usually through a series of peaceful stages.

Finance: The study of funds management or the allocation of assets and liabilities over time under conditions of certainty and uncertainty.

Free Trade: A policy by which a government does not discriminate against imports or interfere with exports by applying tariffs (to imports) or subsidies (to exports) or quotas.

Have-nots: One with little or no material wealth. Economically disadvantaged people.

Haves: Wealthy or privileged.

Holistic: Relating to or concerned with wholes or with complete systems rather than the analysis of treatment of, or dissection into, parts.

Imperialism: It occurs when a strong nation takes over a weaker nation or region and dominates its economic, political or cultural life.

Intertextuality: Derived from Lain *intertext*, meaning to intermingle while weaving. It is the shaping of a text meaning by another text - the interdependent ways in which texts stand in relation to one another (as well as to the culture at large) to produce meaning. The theory that a literary work is not simply the product of a single author, but is a product of its relationship to other texts and to the structures of language itself.

Lag: Lag means failing to keep up or fall behind.

Legitimacy: It is a popular acceptance of an authority, usually a governing law or regime.

Liberal: Not limited to or by established, traditional, orthodox, or authoritarian attitudes, views or dogmas; favourable to progress or reform, as in political or religious affairs.

Liminal: Relating to a transitional or initial stage of a process.

Limited Sovereignty: Many representative democracies provide this through referendum, initiative recall or elections (in direct or indirect democracies).

Lumenarchy: It is a term coined by Skolimowski in 2010. It means a socio-cultural and economic system based on wisdom, truth, altruism, goodness, equity, compassion, justice and creativity.

Lumenosophy: It is derived from Latin word *Lumen* meaning light and Greek word *Sophia* meaning wisdom; thus meaning wisdom of light.

Mercantilism: It is the economic doctrine that government control of foreign trade is of paramount importance for ensuring the military security of the country.

Modernism: Modernism, in its broadest definition is modern thought, character or practice.

Mutiny: It is a conspiracy among members of a group of similarly situated individuals (typically members of the military; or the crew or any ship, even if they are civilians) to openly oppose, change or overthrow an authority to which they are subject.

Nation: This may refer to a community of people who share a common language culture, ethnicity, descent or history.

Nirbhaya: It is an inspiration for a movement demanding respect for women.

Oppression: It is the exercise of authority or power in a burdensome, cruel or unjust manner.

Paradigm: A 'typical example or pattern of something, a pattern or model'.

Particularistic: Exclusive attachment to the interests of one group, class, sect, etc. especially at the expense of the community as a whole; the principle of permitting the right to further its own interests or retain its own laws, traditions, etc.

Patrician: This may refer to original aristocratic families of Ancient Rome.

Philosophy: It is the study of general and fundamental problems, such as those connected with reality, existence, knowledge, values, reason, mind and language.

Plebian: The common people of ancient Rome.

Political system: It is a system of politics and government. It is usually compared to the legal system, economic system, cultural system and other social systems.

Popular Sovereignty: A doctrine in a political theory that government is created by and subject to the will of the people.

Post-structuralism: Any of various theories or methods of analysis, deconstruction. It holds that there are many truths that frameworks must become unstable or decentred. It is also concerned with power structures hegemonic and power and how these elements contribute to and/or maintain structures to enforce hierarchy.

Proletariat: Class of wage earners.

Realist: One who is inclined to literal truth and pragmatism.

Resurgence: A rising again into life, activity or prominence.

Revolution: It is a fundamental change in power or organizational structures that take place in a relatively short period or time.

Shetji-bhaji: It refers to bania-brahman classes.

State: An organized community living under a unified political system – the government.

Status quo: A Latin term meaning the existing state of affairs.

Structural Functionalism: A framework for building theory that sees society as a complex system whose parts work together to promote solidarity and stability.

Structure: A fundamental, tangible or intangible notion referring to the recognition, observation, nature and permanence of patterns and relationships of entities.

Sui generis: A Latin phrase meaning 'of its own kind/genus' and hence 'unique in its characteristics'.

Theory: A comparative and rational type of abstract or generalizing thinking, or the results of such thinking. It is a coherent group of tested general propositions, commonly regarded as correct, that can be used as principles of explanation and prediction for a class of phenomena.

Trans: It is a Latin noun or prefix meaning 'across', 'beyond or on the opposite side'.

Value-laden: An author will frequently use emotional language, which is value-laden to sway our opinions.

Bibliography

Primary Sources

Ambedkar, B.R. (1948). *The Untouchables: Who Were They and Why They Became Untouchables*. Delhi: Amrit.

Ambedkar, B.R. (1949). 'Rights of States and Minorities' submitted on 24 March.

Ambedkar, B.R. (1979). *Writings and Speeches*. Bombay: Education Department, Government of Maharashtra. Vol. I.

Ambedkar, B.R. (1986). *Writings and Speeches*. Bombay: Education Department, Government of Maharashtra. Vol. 8.

Ambedkar, B.R. (1987). *Writing and Speeches*. Bombay: Education Department, Government of Maharashtra. Vol. III.

Ambedkar, B.R. (1990). *Yancha Bahishkrit Bharat aur Mukanayk* (Hindi). Bombay: Education Department, Government of Maharashtra.

Bahujan Samaj Se Appeal (n.d.). New Delhi: BSP Central Office (Party Pamphlet).

Bhartiya Dalit Panchayat (n.d.). Party Pamphlet.

BSP Pamphlet (n.d.). Bijnore: Bharatiya Dalit Panchayat.

Census of India (1871–72). General Report.

'Dalit Vikas' (1997). Lucknow. Information and Public Relations Department. 8 June.

Dalit Vikas (1997). Soochna Avam Jansampark Vibhag. Lucknow. June.

Dr Ambedkar International Award for Social Change (1999). New Delhi: Ministry of Social Justice and Empowerment, Government of India.

Gandhi, M.K. (1920). *Young India*. 29 December.

Gandhi, M.K. (1921). *Young India*. 27 April.

Gandhi, M.K. (1936). *Harijan*. 28 November.

Gandhi, M.K. (1971). *Collected Works of Mahatma Gandhi*. Vol. 47. Delhi: Publication Division.

Gandhi, M. K. (1934). *The Harijan*. 20 April.

'Handbook on National Commission for SCs and STs' (2000). Delhi: Loknayak Bhavan.

'India Corruption Study' (2008). Transparency International.

'Kalyan and Vikas Yojna' (n.d.). Lucknow. Minority Welfare and Wakf Department.

'Major Decisions and Achievements of UP Government under the Dynamic Leadership of Mayawati' (1997). Lucknow: Information and Public Relations Department. 27 September.

Manusmriti, 8.417.

Nandy, Ashish (1998). Speech at United Theological College, Bangalore. 29 July.

'Naye Samaj Ki Oor' (1997). Lucknow: Information and Public Relations Department. 8 July.

Ram, Kanshi (n.d.). Swatantra Bharat Mein Bahujan Samaj Ashrit Kyon. Party Booklet.

Srimad Bhagavatam. 11.15.

Vaishistha Dharamasutra. 18.

Secondary Sources

Books/Journals/Newspapers/TV Reports

'A Timely Warning' (1999). *The Hindu*. 16 December.

Abizadeh, A. (2011). 'Hobbes on the Causes of War: A Disagreement Theory'. *American Political Science Review*. 105(2).

Aditya, Bipan Chandra and Mridula Mukherjee (1999). *India After Independence*. Delhi: Viking.

Akhter, Mohammed Jamil (1999). *Iron Lady Ku. Mayawati*. Delhi. Bhujan Sangthak.

Ambedkar, B.R. (1987). 'The Buddha and His Dharma', in V. Moon (ed.). *Dr B.R. Ambedkar, Writings and Speeches*. Bombay: Education Department, Government of Maharashtra. Vol. II.

'American Beauty' (2013). *Sunday Times*. 22 September.

Amin, S. (1976). 'Unequal Development: An Essay on the Social Formations of Peripheral Capitalism'. *New York Monthly Review Press.*

Anand, Mulk Raj and Zelliot, Eleanor (eds) (1992). *An Anthology of Dalit Literature.* Delhi: Gyan.

Ananth, V. Krishna (1999). 'The Dalit Factor They Cannot Do Without'. *The Hindu.* 26 September.

Ananth, V. Krishna (2000). 'Periyar – Defied Yet Diluted'. *The Hindu.* October 1.

'Anna Hazare to Fast at Ralegan Sidhi for Jan Lok Pal Bill' (2013). *Rediff.com News.* 9 December. 13:19 IST.

Antiwal, K.K. (1999). 'He Bheem Tumhara Abhinandan'. *Dalit Darpan.* Dehradun Bharatiya Dalit Academy.

Arendt, Hannah (1961). *Between and Past and Future.* New York: Viking.

Arneil, Barbara (1996). *John Locke and America.* Oxford: Clarendon Press.

'Asaram Chhindwara Ashram Records Say Girl Is Minor: Police' (2013). *The Times of India.* 9 September.

Aschraft, Richard (ed.) (1989). *The Treaties of Civil Government.* London: Routledge.

Ashcraft, R. (1971). 'Hobbes's Natural Man: A Study in Ideology Formation'. *Journal of Politics.* 33.

'Atal Ki Majboori, Mayawati Jaroori'. (2002). *Rashtriya Sahara.* 4 May. Hastshep Page. (Hindi).

Atey, Manohar (1997). *The Editorials of Kanshi Ram.* Part I. Hyderabad: Bahujan Publication.

'Baba Ramdev Meets PM Modi, Yoga Guru Says 'Issues of National Importance Discussed' (2014). *Zee Media Bureau.* 4 November. 20.31 IST.

Bagul, Babuao (ed.) (1981). *Dalit Sahitya Ajche Kranti Vidnayan (Marathi).* Nagpur: Buddhist Publishing House.

Bahujan Samaj Party. (n.d.). New Delhi: ABCDE Publications.

'Be a Child or Dalit Not Both' (1999). *The Pioneer.* April 14.

Bechain, Sheoraj (2000). 'Why Not Let Us Speak?'. *The Pioneer.* 30 January, Millenium.

Berlin, Isaiah (1967). *Karl Marx: His Life and Environment.* New York: Time Inc Book Division.

Bhambhri, C.P. (1999). 'Dialectics of Caste and Casteism'. *Economic and Political Weekly*. XXXIV (36). 4 September.

Bhegaonkar, Dinbandhu (1992). *Buddha-Palana*. Bhimnagar: Akola Tathagat Publication.

Bhosale, B.V. (2001). 'Issues of Mobilisation for Scheduled Castes in Maharashtra: A Case Study of Charmakars'. Paper presented at a seminar in University of Pune.

'Black Money: Unhappy Anna Hazare Threatens Stir against Centre' (2014). *bing.com/news*. 28 October.

Bloom, A. (1991). *Introduction to Rousseau, J.J. Emile (1762)*. London: Penguin.

Bornschier, V. and C. Dunnchase (1985). *Transnational Corporations and Underdevelopment*. New York: Praeger.

Bose, Devbrata (1968). *The Problems of Indian Society*. Bombay: Popular.

Bottomore, T. (1993). *Elites and Society* (2nd ed.). London: Routledge.

Bottomore, Tom (ed.) (1998). *A Dictionary of Marxist Thought*. Oxford: Blackwell.

Burke, Jason (2007). *Al-Qaeda*. London: Penguin.

Burleigh, Michael (2009). *Blood and Rage: A Cultural History of Terrorism*. New York: Harper Collins Publishers.

Burnham, J. (1960). *The Managerial Revolution*. Bloomington: Indiana University Press.

Byres, T.J. (1988). 'Charan Singh (1902–1987): An Assessment'. *Journal of Peasant Studies (JPS)*. 15(2).

Huntington, Cairns and Edith Hamilton (eds). (1961). *The Collected Dialogues of Plato*. Princeton: Princeton University Press.

Callinicos, Alex (1983). *The Revolutionary Ideas of Karl Marx*. Bloomsbury. London: Book Marks.

'Capital Corruption: Child Labour in India' (n.d.). *Bachpan Bachao Andolan*. Delhi. info@bha.org.in.

Cassinelli, C.W. (1953). 'The Law of Oligarchy'. *American Political Science Review*. 47.

Caws, P. (ed.). *The Causes of Quarrel: Essays on Peace, War and Thomas Hobbes*. Boston: Beacon Press.

Chakravarty, Nikhil (1991). 'Mandal Report, Narasimha Rao and V.P. Singh'. *Mainstream*. XXIX(50). 5 October.

Chandra, Kanchan (1997). 'Party Strategies in the UP Assembly Elections 1996'. *Economic and Political Weekly*. 1 February.

Chandra, Kanchan (1999). 'Mobilizing the Excluded'. *The Seminar* – 471. November.

Charlotte, Chaclotte Vandeville (1997). *A Weaver Named Kabir*. Delhi: OUP.

Chattopadhyaya, Deviprasad (1980). *Lokayta: A Study in Ancient Indian Materialism*. Fifth Edition. Delhi: People's Publishing House.

Chauhan, K.S. (2000). 'In Search of Justice'. *The Pioneer*. Millennium.

Cooper, John M. and D.S. Hutchinson (1997). *Plato, Complete Works*. Hackett.

Cooper, Lane (1960). *The Rhetoric of Aristotle*. New Jersey. Prentice Hall Inc.

Crawley, W.F. (1971). 'Kisan Sabha and Agrarian Revolt in the United Provinces 1920–21'. *Modern Asian Studies*. 5(2).

Dahl, Robert A. (1961). 'The Behavioural Approach in Political Science: Epitaph for a Monument to a Successful Protest'. *American Political Science Review*. December. 55(4).

Das, Arvind (2000). 'Silence of the Wolves'. *The Pioneer Magazine*. 30 January.

Dasgupta, Susmita (2001). 'The Politics of Mobilization of the Backward Classes'. Presented at a seminar at the University of Pune.

De, Barun (1977). 'A Historiographical Critique of Renaissance: Analogues for 19th Century India', in Barun De (ed.). *Perspectives in Social Sciences* I. Delhi: OUP.

Deegwal, Ramesh (1997). 'Dr Bhimrao Ambedkar'. *Dalit Sopan*. Fatehabad: Bhartiya Dalit Sahitya Academy. 28–29 June.

Deleury, Guy A. (1960). *The Cult of Vithoba*. Pune: Deccan College Post-graduate Research Institute.

Deshi, A.K. and Singh, H. (1995). 'Education, Labour Market Distortions and Relative Earning of Different Religious Caste Categories in India. *Canadian Journal of Development Studies*. December 21.

Desai, I.P. (1985). *Caste, Caste Conflict and Reservation*. Delhi: Eastern.

Devi, Vasanthi (2000). 'Dalits and the State'. *Frontline*. 21 July.

Dhar, Hiranmay (1992). 'Escalating Violence on Harijans'. *Economic and Political Weekly*. XXXVII(38). 19 September.

Dhasal, Namdev (1975). *Golpitha*. Translated by D.B. Karnik. Pune. Nilkanth Prakashan.

Dirks, Nicholas B. (2001). *Castes of Mind*. USA: Princeton University Press.

Diwaka, Ranganata R. (ed.) (1968). *Karnataka through the Ages*. Mysore: Government of Karnataka Publication.

Dobbs, Darrell's (1996) article. 'Family Matters: Aristotle's Appreciation of Women and the Plural Structure of Society'. *American Political Science Review*. 90(1).

Dogans, Mattei (2003). 'Conceptions of Legitimacy', in Mary Hawkesworth and Maurice Kogan (ed.). *Encyclopedia of Government and Politics*. Second Edition. Vol. 2. London. Routledge.

Douglas, Martin (2003). 'Gabriel A. Almond, 91. Political Scientist.' *New York Times*. 13 January.

Dubey, Abhay Kumar (2001). 'Anatomy of Dalit Power Player: A Study of Kanshi Ram' in Ghanshyam Shah (ed.) (2001). *Dalit Identity and Politics*. Delhi. Sage.

Dubois, W.E.S. (1918). *Black Folk, Then and Now*. New York: Albany.

Dunn, John (1969). *The Political Thought of John Locke*. Cambridge University Press.

Dutt, R.C. (1993). 'The Mandal Commission'. *Mainstream*. 13 February.

Dyzenhaus, D. and T. Poole (eds.). (2013). *Hobbes and the Law*. Cambridge: Cambridge University Press.

Easton, David (1962). 'Introduction: The Current Meaning of "Behaviouralism"', in James Charlesworth (ed.). *Political Science*. Philadelphia: American Academy of Political and Social Science.

Encyclopaedia Britannica Inc. 2012. Web. 2 December.

Ezekiel, I.A. (1971). 'Ambedkar the Social Revolutionary'. *Times Weekly*. 11 April.

Fairclough, Norman (2003). *Analysing Discourse: Textual Analysis for Social Research*. New York. Routledge.

'Fight Must Be for Political Power' (2000). *The Pioneer*. 30 January. The New Millennium.

'Five Convicted, Sentenced in Gurgaon Kidney Scam' (2013). *The Tribune*. 23 March. Chandigarh.

'Four Charged in Mumbai Photojournalist's Gangrape Case'. (2013). *The Times of India*. 19 September.

Frankel, Francine (1977). 'Problems of Correlating Electoral and Economic Variables: An Analysis of Voting Behaviour and Agrarian Modernisation in UP', in M. Weiner and J.D. Fields (eds.). *Electoral Politics in the Indian States*. Vol. 3. Impact of Modernisation. Delhi: Manohar.

Friedlander, P.G. (1987). 'An Introduction to Ravidas'. SOAS Seminar. December.

Frontline (1999). 5 November.

Gaikwad, S.M. (1998). 'Ambedkar and Indian Nationalism'. *Mainstream*. Vol. XXXIII, No. 10, March 7.

Galanter, Marc (1989). 'Group Membership and Group Preferences in India', in *Law and Society in Modern India*. Delhi: Oxford University Press.

Gandhi, Mahatma (1929). *Young India*. 11 July. Quoted in Mahatma Gandhi (1964). 'All Are Equal in the Eyes of God'. Delhi: Publication Division, Ministry of Information and Broadcasting.

Gandhi, M.K. (1971). *Collective Works of Mahatma Gandhi*. Delhi: Publication Division. Vol. 47.

Ganvir, Ratnakar (1981). *Bahishkrit Bharatatil Dr Ambedkar auche sfut Lekh* (Marathi). Bhusawal: Ratnamitra Prakashan.

Gautam, M.B. (1976). 'The Untouchable Movement in Andhra Pradesh'. Hyderabad. Harijan Conference Souvenir APSH.

Ghatak, B. (ed.) (1999). *Dr Ambedkar's Thought*. Delhi: A.P.H. Publishing House.

Ghatak, B.K. (ed.) (1977). *Dr Ambedkar Thought*. Delhi: A.P.H.

Ghurye, G.S. (1957). *Caste and Class in India*. Bombay: Popular.

Gokhale, Jayashree-Turner (1981). 'Bhakti or Vidroha: Continuity and Change in Dalit Sahitya'. In Jayant Lele (ed.). *Tradition and Modernity in Bhakti Movement*. Leiden: E.J. Brill.

Gore, M.S. (1993). *The Social Context of an Ideology (Ambedkar's Social and Political Thought)*. Delhi: Sage.

Gokhale, Jayashree (1993). From Concessions to Confrontation: The Politics of an Indian Untouchability Community. Bombay. Popular.

Gokhale, Jayashree – Turner (1981). 'Bhakti or Vidroha: Continuity and Change in Dalit Sahitya', in Jayant Lele (ed.). *Tradition and Modernity in Bhakti Movement*. Leiden: E.J. Brill.

Gooptu, Nandini (1993). 'Caste and Labour: Untouchable Social Movements in Urban UP in the Early Twentieth Century', in Peter Robb (ed.). *Dalit Movement and the Meanings of Labour in India*. Delhi: OUP.

Grimsley, R. (1973). *The Philosophy of Rousseau*. Oxford: Oxford University Press.

Guha, Ranjit (1983). *Elementary Aspects of Peasants Insurgence in Colonial India*. London: Oxford.

Gupta, G.V. (2000). 'A Can-Do Canadian Reformer'. *The Sunday Tribune*. 6 February.

Gupta, S.K. (1985). *The Scheduled Castes in Modern Indian Politics: Their Emergence as a Modern Power*. Delhi: Manohar.

Gupta, Shaibal (1998). 'From Untouchable to Dalit'. *Biblio: A Review of Books*. III (11/12), November–December. (Book Review).

Guru, Gopal (1992). 'Dalit Movement in India'. Paper presented at a seminar organised by Bombay Vikas Adhyyan Kendra. August.

Guru, Gopal (1993). 'Dalit Movement in Mainstream Sociology'. *Economic and Political Weekly*. XXVIII(14). 3 April.

Guru, Gopal (1998). 'The Politics of Naming'. *Seminar* 471. November.

Guru, Gopal (2001). 'The Interface between Ambedkar and Dalit Cultural Movement in Maharashtra', in Ghanshyam Shah (ed.). *Dalit Identity and Politics*. New Delhi: Sage.

Guru, Gopal (2001a). 'The Language of Dalit-Bahujan Political Discourse', in Ghanshyam Shah (ed.). *Dalit Identity and Politics*. New Delhi: Sage.

Guru, Gopal (2002). 'Rushing or Reaching?' *Biblio*. September–October. (Book Review)

Guru, Gopal and V. Geetha (2000). 'New Phase of Dalit-Bahujan Activity'. *Economic and Political Weekly*. XXV(3). 15–21 January.

Hanagan, P. Michael (1994). 'Class', in Peter N. Stearns (ed.). *Encyclopedia of Social Theory*. London: Taylor and Francis.

Handy, Charles (1993). *Understanding Organization* (4th ed.). London: Penguin.

Hansen, Lene (2011). 'Poststructuralism', in John Baylis, Steve Smith and Patrica Owens (eds). *The Globalisation of World Politics*. New York: Oxford.

Hanton, Rosalind O' (1985). *Caste, Conflict and Ideology*. Delhi: Orient Longman.

Harrison, Selig (1960). *India: The Most Dangerous Decades*. Madras: Oxford.

Hasan, Zaheer (1986). *Gandhiji and Harijans*. Delhi: Shree.

Hasan, Zoya (2001). 'Transfer of Power Politics of Mass Moblisation in UP'. *Economic and Political Weekly*. XXXVI(46/47). 24–30 November.

Hasan, Zoya (2002). 'Representation and Redistribution: The New Lower Caste Politics of North India', in Zoya Hasan (ed.). *Parties and Party Politics in India*. New Delhi: Oxford University Press.

Haslip, Susan (2003). 'Aristotle's Theory of the Good Life: A Consideration of the Role of Luck in Good Life and the Concept of Self-sufficiency'. *Quodibet Journal*. 5(1). January.

'Health Scan: Former CMO, Sachan Booked'. (2011). *Hindustan Times*. 4 August.

Hero, Dilip (1982). *The Untouchables of India*. London. The Minority Rights Group. Translated by Gauri Deshpande.

Hess, Linda (1983). *The Bijak of Kabir*. San Francisco: North Point Press.

Hobsbawn, Eric (2011). *How to Change the World: Tales of Marx and Marxism*. London: Little Brown.

Hoffman, Bruce (2006). *Inside Terrorism*. (Second Edition). New York: Columbia University Press.

Hoffman, C.B. (1962). *The Political Theory of Possessive Individualism*. Oxford. Oxford University Press.

Huff Post Politics (2014). 'More Countries Join Fight against ISIS' (Reuters). 15 November.

Hymans, Jacques E.C. (2010).'India between "Soft State" and "Soft Power".' in *India in Transition* published by Center for the Advanced Study of India (CASI) of the University of Pennsylvania. 19 January.

IDSN (2014). International Dalit Solidarity Network. October. *Newsletter on Caste Discrimination*.

Ilaiah, Kancha (1991). 'Gautam Budha as a Political Philosopher'. Ph.D Thesis, Chapter 4. Department of Political Science, Osmania University, Hyderabad.

Ilaiah, Kancha (1994). 'BSP and Caste as Ideology'. *Economic and Political Weekly*. XXXIX(12). 19 March.

Ilaiah, Kancha (2001), 'Dalitism versus Brahminism: The Epistemological Conflict in History', in Ghanshyam Shah (ed.). *Dalit Identity and Politics*. New Delhi. Sage.

'In Ambedkar's Country, D Still Can't Enter Temples' (2000). *The Hindustan Times*. 14 April.

'India Has 50 per cent of the World Modern Slaves' (2013). *The Times of India*. 29 October.

'Indian Official Diplomat's Arrest in NYC Barbaric' (2013). Associated Press. 29 December.

Introduction to Apastamba (Hindu Scriptures Website).

Iqbal, Syed (1998). 'The Dalit Dilemma'. *One India One People*.

'ISIS Beheads US Aid Worker, 14 Syrians' (2014) *Hindustan Times*. 17 November.

Issac, Harold (1964). *India's Ex-Untouchables*. Bombay: Asia Publishing House.

Issac, Harold (1965). *Ex-Untouchables*. Bombay: Asia Publication.

Jafferlot, Christophe (2002). *India's Silent Revolution: The Rise of Lower Castes in North India*. Delhi: Permanent Black.

Jain, Meenakshi (1996). 'Backward Castes and Social Change in Uttar Pradesh and Bihar'. In M.N. Srinivas (ed.). (1996). *Caste: Its 20th Century Avtar*. Delhi: Viking.

Jain, Ravindra K. (1996). 'Hierarchy, Hegemony and Dominance'. *Economic and Political Weekly*. 27 January.

Jain, Sobhangmal (1998). 'A Scheduled Injustice'. *The Hindustan Times*. 29 November.

James, Paul (1997). 'Post-Dependency: The Third World in an Era of Globalism and Late Capitalism'. *Alternatives: Social Transformation and Human Governance*. 22. 2 November.

Jatav, D.R. (1965). *The Social Philosophy of B.R. Ambedkar*. Agra: Phoenix.

Jatav, D.R (1998). *Ambedkar Study in Society and Politics*. Jaipur: National.

Jayal, Nirja Gopal and Sudha Pai (2001). *Democratic Governance in India: Challenges of Poverty, Development and Identity*. Delhi: Sage.

Jeffrey, Craig (2000). 'Democratisation without Representation'. *Political Geography*. 19(8). November.

Jordens, J.F.T. (1987). *Dayanand Saraswati: His Life and Ideas*. Delhi: Oxford University Press.

Joshi, Barbara (1987). 'Recent Developments in India – Regional Mobilisation of Dalit Protest in India'. *South Asia Bulletin. 7.*

Joshi, Barbara R. (1982). *Democracy in Search of Equality.* Delhi: National.

Joshi, Barbara R. (1986). *Untouchable: Voice of the Dalit Liberation Movement.* New Delhi: Select Book Service Syndicates.

Joshi, Manoj (2013). 'The Fumbling Soft State: Despite Its Size and Economy, India Looks Like a Pitiable Giant in Neighbourhood'. *Mail Today*. Delhi. 13 January. 15.48 IST.

Juergensmeyer, Mark (1982). *Religion as a Social Vision: The Movement Against Untouchability in the 20th Century Panjab.* Berkeley: University of California Press.

Jurgensmeyer, Mark (1988). *Religious Rebels in the Punjab: The Social Vision of Untouchables*. Delhi: Ajanta.

Kagzi, Mangal Chander Jain (1976). *Segregation and Untouchability Abolition*. Delhi: Metropolitan.

Kamble, Ramesh (1998). 'Dalit Interpretation of Society'. *Seminar.* 471.

Karnataka Through Ages (1968). Bangalore. Government of Karnataka Publication.

Karve, Irawati (1988). 'On the Road: A Mahrashtrian Pilgrimage', Eleanor Zelliot and Maxine Berntsen (eds.). *The Experience of Hinduism: Essays on Religion in Maharashtra*. Albany: State University of New York Press.

Kasbe, Raosaheb (1985). *Ambedkar and Marx.* Pune: Sugawa. (Marathi).

Kavoori, Purnendu S. (2002). 'The Varna Trophic System'. *Economic and Political Weekly*, Vol. XXXVII, No. 12, March 23–29.

Keer, Dhanajay (1962). *Dr Ambedkar: Life and Mission*. Bombay: Popular.

'Kejriwal Takes Oath as Delhi's Youngest CM' (2013). *Yahoo India News*. 28 December.

Khan, Mumtaz Ali (1998). *Scheduled Castes and Their Status in India*. Delhi: Uppal.

Khare, R.S. (1984). *The Untouchable as Himself: Ideology, Identity and Pragmatism among the Lucknow Chamars*. Cambridge: Cambridge University Press.

Koenaad (1993). *Dr Ambedkar: A True Aryan*. Delhi: Voice of India.

Kotani, H. (ed.). (1997). *Caste System: Untouchability and the Depressed*. Delhi: Manohar.

Kothari, Rajni (1994). 'Rise of Dalits and the Renewed Debate on Caste'. *Economic and Political Weekly*. XXIX(26) 25 June.

Krant, Richard (ed.) (1992). *The Cambridge Companion to Plato*. Cambridge.

Kshirsagar, R.K. (1994). *Dalit Movement in India and Its Leaders*. Delhi: M.D. Publications.

Kuber, W.N. (1973). *Ambedkar: A Critical Study*. New Delhi: People's Publishing House.

Kumar, Narendra (2000). 'Dalit and Shudra Politics and Anti-Brahman Movement'. *Economic and Political Weekly*. 4 November.

Kumar, Nirmal (1992). 'Gandhi's Struggle Against Communalism and Casteism'. *Mainstream*. XXX(51). 10 October.

Kumar, Pradeep (1994). 'Backwards Among the Backwards'. *Mainstream*. 8 January.

Kumar, Pradeep (1998). 'Quest for Power: Oppositional Movements and Post-Congress Politics in Uttar Pradesh'. *Seminar 471*. November. (Book Review).

Kumar, Pradeep (1998a). 'Understanding Political Strategies: The BSP'. *Politics India*. June.

Kumar, Pradeep (1999), 'Bahujan Samaj Party Breaking Ground Realities in Uttar Pradesh–II'. *Mainstream*. 8 May.

Kumar, Pradeep (1999a). 'BSP Breaking Ground Realities in Uttar Pradesh'. *Mainstream*. 1 May.

Kumar, Pradeep (1999b). 'Dalits and the Bahujan Samaj Party in Uttar Pradesh: Issues and Challenges'. *Economic and Political Weekly*. 3 April.

Kumar, Pradeep (2001). 'Dalit Politics in Contemporary Uttar Pradesh'. Abstract of paper presented at a seminar. Panjab University, Chandigarh. 27–28 February.

Kumar, Pradeep (2001). 'Identifying Real Backwards and Dalits'. *The Tribune*. 17 October.

Kumar, Pradeep (2001a). 'Reservation within Reservation'. *Economic and Political Weekly*. XXXVI(37). 15 –21 September.

Kumar, Raj (1996). 'Relevance of Ambedkarism in India'. *Mainstream*. XXXIV(24). 18 May.

Kumar, Suresh (1997). 'The Dalit Situation'. *Mainstream*. XXXV(36). 16 August.

Kumar, Suresh (2001). 'Interrogating or Affirming Modernity in Emancipatory Project: B.R. Ambedkar in Perspective'. Paper presented in the seminar on Social Oppression and the Emancipatory Project. 27–28 February. Panjab University, Chandigarh.

Kumar, Vivek (2001). 'Political Utility of Dalits'. *The Pioneer*. 15 February, Editor Page.

Kumar, Vivek (2002). 'Dalit Utthan Ke Liye Satta Zaroori'. *Rashtriya Sahara*. 4 May. Hastshep Page. (Hindi).

Kumar, Vivek and Uday Sinha (2001). *Dalit Assertion and Bahujan Samaj Party: A Perspective from Below*. Lucknow: Bahujan Sahitya Sansthan Publishers.

Kunhappa, Murkot (1982). *Sree Narayana Guru*. Delhi: National Book Trust.

Lasllett, Peter (ed.) (1960). *Locke's Two Treaties of Government*. Cambridge: Cambridge University Press.

Lerch, Jen (1998). 'Agricultural Labours, the State and Agrarian Transition in Uttar Pradesh'. *Economic and Political Weekly*. XXXII (13). 26 March–3 April.

Limaye, Madhu (1988). *Birth of Non-Congressism*. New Delhi: B.R. Publishers.

Lindley, Mark (2004). 'Changes in Mahatma Gandhi's Views on Caste and Intermarriage'. Turkish University Academic Web Journal.

Linell, Per (1998). Discourse Across Boundaries: On Recontextualizations and the Blending of Voices in Professional Discourse. Text 18.

Lipset, M. Seymour (1962). 'Introduction', in Robert Michels (ed.). *Political Parties: A Sociological Study of the Oligarchcal Tendencies of Modern Democracy*. New York: Free Press.

Littmann, Mark, Espenak, Fred, and Willox, Ken (2008). *Totality: Eclipses of the Sun*. Oxford: Oxford University Press.

Lloyd, S.A. (ed.) (2001). 'Special Issue on Recent Work on the Moral and Political Philosophy of Thomas Hobbes'. *Pacific Philosophical Quarterly*. 82(3/4).

Lobo, Lancy (2001). 'Vision, Illusions and Dilemmas of Dalit Christians', in Ghanshyam Shah (ed.). *Dalit Identity and Politics*. Delhi: Sage.

Lochan, Rajiv (1999). 'A Different Kind of Attack on Dalits'. *The Tribune*. 14 November. (Book Review).

Lockhart, Charles (1993). 'Gabriel Almond', in G. Utter and C. Lockhart (eds.). *American Political Scientists: A Dictionary*. Greenwood Press.

Lolordo, Antonia (2010). 'Person, Substance, Mode and 'the Moral Man' in Locke's Philosophy'. *Canadian Journal of Philosophy*. 40 (4).

Lorenzen, David (1981). 'The Kabir Panth Heretics to Hindus', in D.N. Lorenzen (ed.). *Religious Change and Cultural Domination*. Mexico City: El Colegio de Mexico.

Lynch, Oven M. (1974). *The Politics of Unouchability*. Delhi: National Publishing House.

Lynch, Owen (1969). *Politics of Untouchability, Social Mobility and Change in a City of India*. Columbia: Columbia University Press.

Macpherson, C.B. (1962). *The Politiical Theory of Possessive Individualism*. Oxford: Oxford University Press.

Mahar, Michael (1972) (ed.). *Untouchability in Contemporary India*. Tucson: University of Arizona Press.

'Maid Murder Case: Court Asks Tihar to Place Jagriti's Reports' *Zee News*. 9 October 2014. 19.05 IST.

Malik, Ashok (1999). 'Doyam Darje Ki Rani'. *India Today*. 29 September.

Mallik, Basant Kumar (1991). 'Ambedkar and His Movement for Social Equality'. *Mainstream*. XXIX(25). 13 April.

Mallik, Basanta Kumar (1988). 'Marx and Ambedkar: A Comparative Study'. *Mainstream*. XXVI(28). 23 April.

Mallik, Basanta Kumar (1992). 'Ambedkar as a Builder of Modern India'. *Mainstream*. XXX(25). 11 April.

'Manual Scavenging Figures Shocking, Says Jairam'. *The Hindu*. 10 June 2012.

Martinelli, Claudio (2009). 'Gaetano Mosca's Political Theories: A Key to Interpret the Dynamics of Power'. *Italian Journal of Public Law*. I.

Masselos, Jim (1983). 'Jobs and Jobbery: The Sweeper in Bombay under the Raj'. *The Indian Economic and Social History Review*. 19(2).

Maurya, C.L. (1996). BSP Supremo Kanshi Ram Press Ke Samne. Allahabad: Kushwali.

'Mayawati Plays Sister to Jehrana's Dalit' (2002). *Indian Express*. June 16.

Mayawati (2000). *Bahujan Samaj Aur Uski Rajneeti*. Lucknow. BSP Publishers. Prastavana, 9. (Hindi).

Mehta, Uday (1998). 'Social Transformation in India'. *One India, One People*. Vol 2/3. October.

Mehta, Uday (1998). 'Untouchability and Social Transformation in India'. *One India One People*. October.

Melzer, A.M. (1990). *The National Goodness of Man: On the System of Rousseau's Thought*. Chicago. Chicago University Press.

Mendelson, Oliver and Marika Vicziany (2000). *The Untouchables: Subordination, Poverty and the State in Modern India*. Delhi. Cambridge University Press.

Menon, Girish (2000). 'Creamy Layer Issue: NSS Cautions Kerala Government'. *The Hindu*. 22 January.

Miller, J. (1984). *Rousseau: Dreamer of Democracy*. London: Yale University Press.

Mishra, Amaresh (1996). 'Backwards and Dalits Take a Backseat'. *Economic and Political Weekly*. Vol. XXXI, no. (39) 29 September.

Mishra, Amaresh (1998). 'UP Order Behind Anarchy'. *Economic and Political Weekly*. XXXIII(18). 2 May.

Mitra, Subrata Kumar (ed.) (1990). *Politics of Positive Discrimination*. Bombay: Popular.

Moffatt, Michael (1979). *An Untouchable Community in South Asia*. USA: Princeton University Press.

Mohan, B. (1972). *India's Social Problems: Analyzing Basic Issues*. Allahabad: India International Publications.

Moon, Vasant (ed.) (1987). *Dr Bhimrao Ambedkar. Writing and Speeches*. Bombay: Education Department, Government of Maharashtra. Vol. III.

Moon, Vasant (ed.) (1990). *Dr B.R. Ambedkar. Writing and Speeches*. Bombay. Education Department, Government of India, Maharashtra. Vol. IV.

Mukherjee, Chandan N. Krishnaji, and Preet Rustogi (2001). 'Crimes and Women in India'. *Economic and Political Weekly*. XXXVI(43). 27 October.

Murthy, B.S. (1976). *Depressed and Oppressed (Forever in Agony)*. Delhi: S. Chand and Co.

Murugkar, Lata (1988). 'Dalit Literacy Movement in Maharashtra and Dalit Movement'. Presented in a seminar on Dalit Literature. Surat: Centre for Social Studies.

Murugkar, Lata (1991). *Dalit Panther Movement in Maharashtra (A Sociological Appraisal)*. Bombay: Popular Prakashan.

Mustafa, Seema (1996). *The Lonely Prophet: A Political Biography of V.P. Singh*. Delhi: Wiley Eastern.

Naimishrai, Mohan Das (2002). 'Ek Raja Ka Dalit Goshna Patra'. *Rashtriya Sahara*. Hastshep. 26 January (Hindi).

Nair, K.P. Prabhakaran (1999). 'Manu and Mandal'. *The Hindu*. 3 August.

Nalapat, Monu (1998). 'Dalit vs the Rest'. *One India One People*. Vol. 2/3.

Nandy, Ashis (1988). Speech at United Theological College, Bangalore. 29 July.

Narayan, Badri (2001). 'Dalit Consciousness and Popular Booklets'. Paper presented at seminar on 'Social Oppression and the Emancipatory Project' held at Panjab University, Chandigarh. 27–29 February.

Nath, Priti (2001). 'Politics of Racial Transformation'. Paper presented at a seminar 'Social Oppression and the Emancipatory Project' at Panjab University. 27–28 February.

Nath, Priti (2009). 'Cultural Subordination and Dalit Challenge'. Research paper presented at a national level seminar on 'Dalits in Historical Perspective in North Western India' at Government College, Chandigarh. 13–14 February.

Nath, Priti (2009a). Paper presented at a state-level seminar on 'Post-colonial Literature: Revival of Cultural Identity' at Government College, Panchkula. 18 November.

Nath, Priti (2010). 'Dalit Women: Changing Political Face'. Research paper presented at a national level seminar on 'Situating Women in History, Culture and Polity of North Western India' held in PG Government College, Chandigarh. 15–16 February.

Nath, Priti (2010a). 'Dalits of North Western India: Cultural Subordination and Dalit Challenge' in Benudhar Patra and Kanta Singhania. *Dalits in Historical Perspective in North-Western India*. Delhi: Pratibha Prakashan.

Nath, Priti (2015). 'Post-Colonial Literature Revival of Cultural Identity', in Sarika Dubey (ed.) *Women Empowerment Challenges of the Millennium*. Delhi: Adhyayan.

Nath, Trilok (1987). *Politics of Depressed Classes*. Delhi: Deputy.

Nath, Tripti (2011). 'India's Shunned Latrine Cleaners Toil Despite Ban'. We.News. 6 February.

NDTV (2014). 8 January.

Neale, Walter (1962). *Economic Change in Rural India Land Tenure and Reform in UP 1800–1955*. New Haven: Yale University Press.

Nigam, Aditya (2002). 'In Search of a Bourgeoisie'. *Economic and Political Weekly*. Vol. XXXVII, no. 13, March 30.

Nimbalkar, Waman (1973). *Gaokushabaheril Kavita*. Translated by G. Smith and E. Zelliot. Aurangabad: Asmitadarsh Prakashan.

Nussbaum, C. Martha (1986). *Fragility of Goodness*. Cambridge: Cambridge University Press.

O'Hanton, Rosalind (1985). *Caste, Conflict and Ideology*. Delhi: Orient Longman.

'Obama's Brother Writes about Domestic Abuse' (2013). *The Times of India*. 20 December.

Olivelle, Patrick (2004). *The Law Code of Manu*. New York: OUP.

Omvedt, Gail (1992). *Dalit Visions: The Anti-caste Movement and the Construction of an Indian Identity*. Delhi: Orient Longman.

Omvedt, Gail (1994). *Dalits and the Democratic Revolution*. Delhi. Sage.

Omvedt, Gail (1994a). 'Kanshi Ram and the BSP', in K.L. Sharma (ed.). *Caste and Class in India*. Jaipur: Rawat Publications.

Omvedt, Gail (1994b). *Dr Ambedkar and Dalit Movement in Colonial India*. New Delhi: Sage.

Omvedt, Gail (1995). *Dalit Vision*. New Delhi: Orient Longman.

Omvedt, Gail (1996). 'Ambedkar and Economics'. *Fourth World*. 3(1).

Omvedt, Gail (1998). 'Peasants Dalits and Women: Democracy and India's New Social Movements', in M. Mohanty, Partha N. Mukerji with Olle Tornquist. *People's Rights Social Movements and State in the Third World*. New Delhi: Sage.

Omvedt, Gail (1999). 'Dalits and Election I', *The Hindu*. 5 November.

Omvedt, Gail (1999a). 'Dalits and Election II', *The Hindu*. 6 January.

Omvedt, Gail (1999b). 'The Dravidian Movement II'. *The Hindu*. 22 June.

Omvedt, Gail (2000). 'Breaking the Majority's Tyranny II'. *The Hindu*. 24 August.

Omvedt, Gail (2002). 'Udaarikaran Se Hogi Daliton Ki Mukti'. *Rashtriya Sahara*. January 26, Hastshep, (in Hindi).

Omvedt, Gail (2000a). 'The Purpose of Reservation I'. *The Hindu*. 24 March.

Omvedt, Gail (2000b). 'The Purpose of Reservation II'. *The Hindu*. 25 March.

Omvedt, Gail (2001). 'Ambedkar and After: The Dalit Movement in India', in Ghanshyam Shah (ed.). *Dalit Identity and Politics*. New Delhi: Sage.

Oommen, T.K. (1990). *Protest and Change: Studies in Social Movements*. New Delhi: Sage.

Oommen, T.K. (1999a). 'Dalit and Production of Knowledge I'. *The Hindu*. 13 September.

Oommen, T.K. (1999b). 'Dalits and Production of Knowledge II'. *The Hindu*. 15 September.

Oommen, T.K. (2000). 'Contours of Mind'. *The Pioneer*. 30 January.

Orr, William G. (1947). *A Sixteenth Century Indian Mystic: Dadu and His Followers*. London: Lutherworth Press.

Padgaonkar, Dileep (1990). 'Ambedkar and Gandhi'. *Mainstream*. XXVIII(26). 21 April.

Pai, Sudha (1997). 'Dalit Assertion in UP'. *Economic and Political Weekly*. 13 September.

Pai, Sudha (1998). 'The BSP in Uttar Pradesh'. *Seminar–471*. November.

Pai, Sudha (1999). 'BSP's New Electoral Strategy Pays Off'. *Economic and Political Weekly*. XXXIV(44). 30 October.

Pai, Sudha (1999). *State Politics: New Dimensions*. New Delhi: Shipra Publications.

Pai, Sudha (2001). 'From Harijan to Dalits Identity Formation, Political Consciousness and Electoral Mobilization of the Scheduled Castes in Uttar Pradesh', in Ghanshyam Shah (ed.). *Dalit Identity and Politics*. New Delhi: Sage.

Pai, Sudha (2001). 'The State, Social Justice, Politics and Dalit Movement: The BSP in UP', in Nirja Gopal Jayal and Sudha Pai (eds.). *Democratic Governance in India*. New Delhi: Sage.

Pai, Sudha (2002). *Dalit Assertion and Unfinished Democratic Revolution: The Bahujan Samaj Party in Uttar Pradesh*. New Delhi: Sage.

Pai, Sudha (2002). *State Politics: New Dimensions*. New Delhi: Shipra Publications.

Pandey, Gyanendra (1978). *The Assembly of Congress in UP 1926–34: A Study of Imperfect Mobilisation*. Delhi: Oxford.

Pandhian, M.S.S. (2002). 'One Step Outside Modernity'. *Economic and Political Weekly*. XXXVII(18). 4–10 May.

Parvarthamha, C. (1984). *Scheduled Castes and Tribes: A Socio-economic Survey*. Delhi: Ashish.

Paswan, Bhaskar Roy (2000). 'Mandal Movement is Dead'. *The Times of India*. 6 July.

Patel, V.T. (ed.). *Studies in Ambedkar*. Delhi: Devika.

Patra, Benudhar and Singhania, Kanta (ed.). (2010). *Dalits in Historical Perspective in North-Western India*. Delhi: Pratibha Prakashan.

Patwardhan, Sunanda (1973). *Change Among India's Harijan*. Delhi: Orient.

Pillai, G.K. (1959). *Origin and Development of Caste*. Delhi: Kitab Mahal.

Prakash, Prem (1997). 'Risky Reservations'. *The Tribune*. 13 August.

Prasad, Chandra Bhan (2000). 'The Fourth World'. *The Pioneer*. 12 October, Op-ed Page,

Prasad, Chandra Bhan and Bechain, Sheoraj Singh (2000). 'Where Non-Dalits Commentators Err'. *The Hindu*. January 4.

Prasad, Guru (1999). 'Jhansi Veerangana Laxmi Bai Nahi Woh Jhalkari Thi'. *Dalit Darpan*. Dehradun. Bharatiya Dalit Academy.

Prasad, Vijay (1996). 'The Untouchable Question'. *Economic and Political Weekly*. 2 March.

Premi, Jai Singh (1999). 'Ansu'. *Dalit Darpan*, Dehradun. Bharatiya Dalit Academy.

Pundir, J.K. (2001). 'Emancipation from Dominant Caste to Fight for Rights – Journey of Backward Caste Mobilization'. Paper presented at a seminar on Social Oppression and Emancipatory Project. Panjab University, Chandigarh. 27–28 February.

'Punjab's Dalits: A Divided House', *Times of India*, 13 November 2014.

Punalekar, S.P. (2001). 'Dalit Literature and Dalit Identity'. In Ghanshyam Shah (ed.). *Dalit Identity and Politics*. New Delhi: Sage.

Pushpendra (1999). 'Dalit Assertion through Electoral Politics'. *Economic and Political Weekly*. XXXIV(36). 4–10 September.

Pushpendra (2001). 'Dalit Assertion Through Electoral Politics', in Ghanshyam Shah (ed.). *Dalit Identity and Politics*. Delhi: Sage.

Raghavan, V. (1966). 'The Great Integrates: The Saint Singers of India'. New Delhi: Ministry of Information and Broadcasting, Government of India.

Rahman, Syed Ubaidur (1998). 'Social Tensions in the Indian Society'. *One India, One People*. October.

Rai, V.K. (1999). 'In Search of a New Balance'. *Economic and Political Weekly*. XXXIV(34/35). 21–27 August.

Raj, Udit (2002). 'An Unholy Alliance'. *Indian Express*. 6 May.

Raja Lakshmi, T.K. (2001). 'Castes and Killings'. *Frontline*. July 20.

Rajan, Ambeth (1994). *My Bahujan Samaj Party*. New Delhi: ABCDE Publications.

Rajeshwar, T.V. (1998). 'The Curse of the Caste System'. *The Hindustan Times*. 22 November.

Rajeshwar, T.V.R (1995). 'Periyar and Struggle for Social Justice'. *The Tribune*. 20 October.

Ralhan, O.P. (ed.) (1987). *The Depressed Classes in India*. Delhi: Gitanjali.

Ram, Kanshi (1982). *The Chamcha Age: The Era of Stooges*. Privately published.

Ram, Nandu (1988). *The Mobile Scheduled Castes: Rise of a New Middle Class*. Delhi: Hindustan.

Ram, Nandu (1995). *Beyond Ambedkar*. Delhi: Har Anand.

Ram, P.R. (1998). 'Purity, Pollution and Quest for Social Justice'. *One India One People*. October.

Ram, Tulsi (1999). 'Antim Daav Hein Rajneetic Asthirtha'. *Rashtriya Sahara*. 4 September (Hindi).

Ramachandran, Shastri (1998). 'Towards a Non-Brahman Millennium: From Iyothee Thass to Periyar'. *Seminar*–471. (Book Review).

Ramaseshan, Radhika (1995). 'Dalit Politics in UP'. *Seminar–425*. January.

Ramaswamy, K. (2000). 'Merit Is No Birth Right'. *The Pioneer*. Millennium.

Rana, Ajit (2000). 'BJP Is an Anti-Dalit Party'. *The Pioneer*. 2 September.

Randeep, Ramesh (2008). 'Indian Police Arrest Suspected Kidney Snatching Gang'. *The Guardian*. 25 January. 12.58 GMT.

Rangarajan, Mahesh (1999). 'The BSP: Dalit Power of the Force'. *The Times of India*. 20 August.

Rao, M. Venugopala (1990). 'Caste War Out in Open'. *Mainstream*. XXVIII(49). 29 September.

Rao, M.S.A. (1982). *Social Movements in India*. Vol. I. Delhi: Manohar.

'Rare Pictures of Sex Assault Accused Narayan Sai' (2013). *India TV Crime Desk*. 24 October. 06:24:10 IST.

Rashtriya Sahara (2002). Hastshep, January 26, (Hindi).

Reddy, B. Krishna (1995). 'Ambedkar and Dalits: An Anthropological Perspective', in V.T. Patel (ed.). *Studies in Ambedkar*. Delhi: Devika.

Reddy, B. Muralidhar (1999). 'Dalit Dynamics at Work'. *The Hindu*. 22 August.

Reep, Ed, (ed.). (2013). 'Men Are the Oppressed Gender'. *The Daily Targum*. 22 April. 12.00 am.

Regan, Sarojin (1976). 'Social Reformers of Andhra Pradesh in the Cause of Harijans Upliftment', in *Andhra Pradesh Harijan Conference Souvenir*. Hyderabad.

Ridgeway, Cecilia L. (2011). *Framed by Gender: How Gender Inequality Persists in the Modern World*. Oxford: Oxford University Press.

Rogers, G.A.J. (ed.). (1995). *Leviathan: Contemporary Responses to the Political Theory of Thomas Hobbes*. Bristol: Thoemmes Press.

Roy, Ramashray and V.B. Singh (1987). *Between Two Worlds: A Study of Harijan Elites*. Delhi: Discovery.

Rudolph, Lloyd I. and Rudolph, Susanne Hoeber (1967). *Modernity of Tradition*. Delhi: Longman.

Russell, Daniel (2004). 'Locke on Land and Labour'. *Philosophical Studies*. 117(1/2).

Sahay, Mohan (1997). 'Dalit Politics: The Relevance of Ambedkar'. *The Statesman*. 19 August.

Sainath, P. (1998). 'Glass Struggle Continues'. *The Hindu*. Sunday Magazine. November 15.

Sainath, P. (1998). 'A Labour of the Unloved'. *The Hindu*. 5 April, Sunday Edition.

Saradmoni, K. (1980). *Emergence of a Slave Caste: Pulayas of Kerala*. Delhi: People's Publishing House.

Schmid, Alex P. (ed.) (2011). *The Routledge Handbook of Terrorism Research*. New York: Routledge.

Seminar–471. 'The Problem'. (1998). November.

Sengupta, Somini and David E. Sanger (2014). *The New York Times*. 29 September.

SEP (Stanford Encyclopedia of Philosophy). First published 22 November 2006. Substantive revision. 3 June 2011.

Shah, Ghanshyam (1988). *Social Movements in India*. New Delhi. Sage.

Shah, Ghanshyam (2001). 'Dalit Movements and the Search for Identity', in Ghanshyam Shah (ed.). *Dalit Identity and Politics*. Delhi: Sage.

Shah, Ghanshyam (2001a). 'Dalit Politics: Has It Reached an Impasse?', in Nirja Gopal Jayal and Sudha Pai (eds.). *Democratic Governance in India*. New Delhi: Sage.

Shah, Ghanshyam (ed.). (2001b). *Dalit Identity and Politics*. New Delhi: Sage.

Shakir, Moin (1980). *Politics of Minorities*. Delhi: Ajanta.

Shannon, Thomas R. (1996). *An Introduction to the World-System Perspective*. Second Edition. Westview Press.

Sharan, Awadhendra (2001). 'Colonialism and the Question of Untouchability'. Paper presented at a seminar on 'Social Oppression and the Emancipatory Project' in Panjab University, Chandigarh. 27–28 February.

Sharma, Subash (1997). 'Divide and Rule'. *India Today*. 31 May.

Shetty, Sadanand A. (1998). 'It is a National Shame'. *One India One People*. Vol. 2/3, October.

Singer M. and B. Cohen (ed.) (1968). *Structure and Change in Indian Society*. Chicago. Aldine.

Singh, Jagpal (1998). 'Ambedkarization and Assertion of Dalit Identity: Socio-Cultural Protest in Meerut District of Western UP' *Economic and Political Weekly*. XXXIII(40). 3–9 October.

Singh, Jagpal (2001). 'Ambedkarization and Dalit Identity: A Case of the BSP'. Paper presented at a seminar on Social Oppression and Emancipatory Project. Panjab University. 27–28 February. Chandigarh.

Singh, K.S. (1995). *The Scheduled Castes*. Delhi: Oxford.

Singh, Mohinder (1947). *The Depressed Classes Their Economic and Social Conditions*. Bombay: Hind Kitab.

Singh, Nirvikar (2010). 'The Trillion-Dollar Question'. *The Financial Express*. 19 December.

Singh, V.B. (1996). Report of National Election Survey Submitted by CSDS to the Indian Council of Social Science Research. New Delhi.

Sonkar, Roop N. (1999). 'Jab Sab Ka Malik Ek Hai'. *Dalit Darpan*. Dehradun: Bharatiya Dalit Academy.

Srinivas, M.N. (1997). 'Varna and Caste', in Dipankar Gupta (ed.). *Social Stratification*. Delhi: Oxford University Press.

Srinivas, M.N. (ed.) (1996). *Caste: Its 20th Century Avatar*. Delhi: Viking.

'States Fudging Data, Taking Money but Not Building Toilets: Jairam Ramesh'. *PTI*. 14 August, 2012. 14.54 IST

Stone, Brewer (1988). 'Institutional Decay and the Traditionalisation of the Congress Party in UP'. *Asian Survey*. 28(10).

Surajbhan (1999). 'Daliton Ko Apne Adhikaron Ke Liye Ladna Hoga'. *Dalit Darpan*. Dehradun: Bhartiya Dalit Academy.

Suresh, V. (1998) 'The Dalit Movement in India', in T.V. Sathyamurthy (ed.). *Religion, Caste, Gender and Culture in Contemporary India*. Delhi: OUP Press.

'Tarun Tejpal and Tehelka's Fall from Grace' (2013). *The Tribune*. 23 November.

'The Dark Side of Asaram Bapu' (2013). *Open*. 9 February.

The Hindu Business Line (2010). 'Black, Bold and Beautiful'. The hindubusinessline.in. 13 August.

The Hindu (1999). 'A Timely Warning'. 16 December.

The Hindu (2000). 'Getting Round the Mandal Verdict'. 15 May.

The Hindustan Times (1991) January 19. Quoted in Ambeth Rajan (1994). *My Bahujan Samaj Party*. Delhi. ABCDE Publication.

The Hindustan Times (1999). New Delhi. 10 October.

The Hindustan Times (2001). 'Murderers Call the Shots'. 2 June.

The Hindustan Times 8 September 2013. p. 1.

The Illustrated Weekly of India (1987), 8 March, quoted in Ambeth Rajan's (1994). *My Bahujan Samaj Party*. New Delhi: ABCDE Publications.

'The Mayawati Enigma' (2002). *The Hindu*. 27 February.

'The Nirbhaya Case: Supreme Court Stays Death Sentence of Two Convicts' (2014). *The Hans India*. 14 July. 07.36 IST.

The Pioneer (1998). 20 February.

The Pioneer (2000). 'Fight Must Be for Political Power'. Millennium.

The Pioneer (2000). 'The Leaders' The New Millennium. 30 January.

'The Problem' (1998). *Seminar* 471.

The Statesman (1997). 'Dalit Agenda to Continue in UP' 21 September.

The Statesman (1997a). 'New Icons of Dalit Movement' 21 September.

The Sunday Observer (1990). 12 August.

The Times of India (1938). February 14.

The Times of India (2014). 5 June.

The Times of India (2014). 12 December.

The Tribune (1994). 6 May

The Tribune (2000). 'Handling the Ambedkar Legacy'. 14 April.

The Tribune (1997). 'Risky Reservations Why Subvert the System'. 13 August.

Thomassen, Bjorn. (2012). 'Toward an Anthropology of Political Revolutions'. *Comparative Studies in Society and History*. 54 (3). pp. 679–706.

Thorat, S.K. and R.K. Deshpande (2001). 'Caste System and Economic Inequality', in Ghanshyam Shah (ed.). *Dalit Identity and Politics*. Delhi: Sage.

Thorat, Sukhadeo. (2002). 'Oppression and Denial: Dalit Discrimination in the 1990s'. *Economic and Political Weekly*. XXXVII(6). 9 February.

Times of India. (2014). 5 June.

Tiwari, Chitra (1963). *Sudras in Manu*. Delhi: Moti Lal Banarsidass.

'Treat Caste on a Par with Racism Apartheid' (2000). *The Hindu*. April 20.

Tripathi, Arun Kumar (2001). 'Dalit Digvijay Aur Agneda'. *Rashtriya Sahara*. August 11, Hastshep (Hindi).

Tripathi, Rebati Ballav (1994). *Dalits: A Sub-human Society*. Delhi: Ashish.

Vakil, A.K. (1991). *Gandhi-Ambedkar Dispute*. Delhi: Ashish.

Varma, Ram Sharan (1999). 'Dalit Sahitya Ki Mool Bhavanayen' (Hindi). *Dalit Darpan*. Dehradun: Bhartiya Dalit Academy.

Varma, Ram Sharan (1999a). 'Takdir Na Badli Daliton Ki'. *Dalit Darpan*. Dehradun: Bharatiya Dalit Academy.

Venkataswamy, P.R. (1955). *Our Struggle for Emancipation*. no. 40. Secunderabad, Ghasmandi Road. Vol. II.

Verma, A.K. (2001). 'UP-BJP's Caste Card'. *Economic and Political Weekly*. XXXVI(48). 1–7 December.

Verma, P.S. (2001). 'Dalit Mobilisation in Punjab'. Paper (abstract) presented in a seminar. Panjab University, Chandigarh. 27–28 February.

Vibhute, K.I. (1993). 'Ambedkar's Sense of Social Justice'. *Mainstream*. XXI(22). 10 April.

Weber, Max (1968). *Economy and Society*, in Guenther Roth and Claus Wittich (eds.). Berkeley: University of California Press.

Wildavsky, Ben (2011). 'Academic Colonialism, False Consciousness and the Western University Ideal'. *The Chronicle of Higher Education*. 4 August.

Willkinson, Steven (2000). 'Indian Consociational Theory and Ethnic Violence'. *Asian Survey*. XI(5).

Wyatt, Andrew (1997). 'BSP Makes a Defining Movement'. *India Today*. 20 January.

Yadav, R.C. and Rajbir Singh (1994). *India's Unequal Citizens*. Delhi: Manohar.

Yadav, Yogendra (1999). 'The Third Electoral System'. *Seminar–480*. August.

Yadav, Yogendra (2000). 'Understanding the Second Democratic Upsurge: Trends of Bahujan Participation in Electoral Politics in the 1990s', in Francine Frankel (ed.). *Transforming India Social and Political Dynamics of Democracy*. Delhi: Oxford. Quoted in R.S. Khare (1984). *The Untouchable as Himself: Ideology, Identity and Pragmitism among the Lucknow Chamars*. Cambridge: Cambridge University Press.

Yevgenia, Yurlova (1991). 'Political Emergence of the Ethno Community'. *Mainstream*. XXXIX(51). 12 October.

Yurlova, Yevgenia (1991). 'Political Emergence of SC Ethno Community'. *Mainstream*. 29(51). 12 October.

Zaidi, A.M. (1986). 'Congress Party Election Manifesto: Lok Sabha Elections 1971', in *Promises to Keep. A Study of the Election Manifestoes of the INC 1937–85*. Delhi: Indian Institute of Applied Research.

Zee Media Bureau (2013). 'What Caused the Kedarnath Tragedy?' 20 June. 13.05 IST.

Zelliot, Eleanor (1972). 'Dalit New Cultural Context for an Old Marathi World'. *Asian Studies*. 11.

Zelliot, Eleanor (1972 a). 'Gandhi and Ambedkar: A Study in Leadership', in Michael Mahar (ed.). *Untouchability in Contemporary India*. Tucson: University of Arizona Press.

Zelliot, Eleanor (1998). 'From Untouchable to Dalit: Essays on the Ambedkar Movement'. Delhi: Manohar.

Zelliot, Eleanor (1998a). 'The Roots of Dalit Consciousness'. *Seminar* 471. November.

Zelliot, Eleanor (2000). 'The Eight-fold Path'. *The Pioneer*. New Millennium.

Zelliot, Eleanor (2001). 'Dalit Trends and Dalit Consciousness', in Nirja Gopal Jayal and Sudha Pai (eds.). *Democratic Governance in India*. New Delhi: Sage.

Zelliot, Eleanor (2001). *From Untouchable to Dalit: Essays on Ambedkar's Movement*. Delhi: Manohar.

Zelliot, Eleanor (2001). 'Gandhi and Ambedkar: A Study in Leadership', in Barbara R. Joshi's (ed.). *Democracy in Search of Equality Untouchable Politics and Indian Social Change*. Delhi: Hindustan.

Websites

https://www.google.co.in/search?q=www.dalitstan.org&oq=www.dalitstan.org&aqs=chrome.69i58j69i57.5100j0j8&sourceid=chrome&es_sm=93&ie=UTF–8

https://www.google.co.in/webhp?sourceid=chrome-instant&ion=1&espv=2&ie=UTF–8#q=www.info%40bha.org.in

www.bing.com/news

www.DalitMarch.org/manualscavenging.html

www.dalits.org

www.dalitwa.org

www.thehindubusinessline.in

Index